Samuel A. Drake

Around the Hub

A Boys' Book about Boston

Samuel A. Drake

Around the Hub
A Boys' Book about Boston

ISBN/EAN: 9783337191979

Printed in Europe, USA, Canada, Australia, Japan

Cover: Foto ©Andreas Hilbeck / pixelio.de

More available books at **www.hansebooks.com**

A Boys' Book about Boston.

BY

SAMUEL ADAMS DRAKE,

AUTHOR OF "OLD LANDMARKS OF BOSTON," "OLD LANDMARKS AND HISTORIC
FIELDS OF MIDDLESEX," "NOOKS AND CORNERS OF THE
NEW-ENGLAND COAST," ETC.

BOSTON:
ROBERTS BROTHERS.
1881.

Copyright, 1881,
BY SAMUEL ADAMS DRAKE.

UNIVERSITY PRESS:
JOHN WILSON AND SON, CAMBRIDGE.

CONTENTS.

I.
THE FIRST INHABITANTS.

The Indians. — Anecdotes illustrating their Manners and Customs. — English vs. Indian Hospitality. — Indians at Boston . . **7**

II.
THE PURITANS HANG UP THEIR HATS.

The First Settlers of Boston. — Who they were. — Winthrop's Company. — Their Location. — Early Houses. — Streets. — Government, etc. **19**

III.
OLD BOSTON NOTIONS.

Drumming for Recruits. — Night Watchmen. — Taverns. — An Unlighted Town. — Mode of Address. — Social Distinctions. — Slaves. — Sunday Observances. — Church Music. — Punishments. — Games. — Curious Regulations. — Education. — Old Superstitions. — Religious Intolerance. — Military Customs. — Arms, Armor, and Dress. — Method of Voting. — Male and Female Dress. — Money. — Household Furniture and Domestic Utensils. — A Puritan Dinner-Table **28**

IV.
FORT HILL, AN INTERLUDE.

The King takes away the Charter. — His New Governor. — The kind of Man Sir Edmund Andros was. — Fort Hill. — The 18th of April, 1689. — The Bostonians rise in Arms. — Andros's Government overthrown. — The New or Province Charter . . **52**

V.
LIBERTY TREE.

Travelling to Town over the Neck. — Old Ways of Travel. — Enoch Brown's House. — The Old Fortifications. — Liberty Tree and Liberty Hall. — Hanging in Effigy. — The Stamp Act. — Rev. Mather Byles **61**

VI.
A TEMPEST IN A BIG TEAPOT.

The Old South Meeting. — The Tea Party. — Boston Harbor a Teapot. — Who Samuel Adams was. — Street Signs and Symbols. — The Province House and Governor General Gage's. — Boston to be starved into Submission 73

VII.
FROM THE OLD CORNER TO KING STREET.

Anne Hutchinson. — The King's Chapel. — An Old-Time Congregation. — Whig and Tory. — King's Chapel Burial Ground. — Court House and Prison. — Legal Punishments. — The Town-House. — A Provincial Congress takes the place of the House of Representatives 88

VIII.
THE ROYAL BEAST SHOWS HIS TEETH.

Arrival of the King's Own. — Camp on the Common. — The Surroundings. — The Great Elm. — Paddock's Mall. — Earl Percy and his Quarters. — John Hancock and his Mansion. — A Boston Rebel. — Officers frightened by Dor-beetles 96

IX.
A GARRISONED TOWN.

More Troops. — Bayonet Rule in Boston. — Paddock's Guns carried off. — A Yankee Marksman 111

X.
FANEUIL HALL AND NEIGHBORHOOD.

Rebellion Advancing. — Brattle Street Church. — The Cradle of Liberty. — The Boston Militia of '75. — Spirited Act of the 'Ancients.' — Boston Stone. — Ben Franklin astonishes the Governor. — The Green Dragon. — Pope Day Celebration. — Hatching Treason. — Gage's Plans frustrated. — Warren and Revere. — The Ride to Lexington 118

XI.

THE OLD NORTH END.

PAGE

Christ Church. — A Visit to Copp's Hill. — The Mathers. — A Distinguished Family. — Charter Street. — Sir Wm. Phips. — Captain Gruchy and his Secret Gallery. — The North Battery. — North Square. — Old Houses. — Sir Charles Frankland's. — Governor Hutchinson's. — Odd Family Names. — Mother Cary 139

XII.

TO ARMS! TO ARMS!

Open Rebellion. — Exodus from Boston. — Daring of the Provincials. — Dorchester vs. Charlestown Heights. — A British Council of War. — A Rebel Ditto. — The First Move. — The Right of Command. — The Stolen March to Breed's Hill . . 156

XIII.

THE SWORD OF BUNKER HILL.

Gage sends Howe to storm the Heights. — The American Defences. — The Redoubt and Rail Fence. — Putnam takes Command. — Stark, Warren, Prescott. — What Each did. — Charlestown burned. — The Battle 169

XIV.

YANKEE DOODLE.

Exhaustion on Both Sides. — Intrenching. — Prospect Hill. — The Provincial Camps 185

XV.

THE NEW ENGLAND ARMY.

The Situation reviewed. — Cambridge. — General Ward's. — The College Halls. — President's House 192

XVI.

WASHINGTON.

Hail to the Chief! — The Washington Elm. — The Army and its Head. — Headquarters. — The Virginia Rifles. — Knox's Mission to Lake Champlain. — Lee and Gates. — Church's Treason. — Gov. Oliver's 203

XVII.

TO ROXBURY TOWN.

Incidents of the Nineteenth of April. — Charles River Redoubts. — Col. Thomas Gardner 223

XVIII.

ROXBURY CAMP AND LINES.

Ward's Headquarters. — High Fort. — The Parting Stone. — Meeting-House Hill. — Roxbury Fort. — General Thomas. — How Cannon-balls were obtained from the Enemy. — The Warren Homestead. — Burying Ground Redoubt. — Skirmishing on the Neck 230

XIX.

ORDERS OF THE DAY.

Dorchester Heights to be occupied. — Preparations. — Boston bombarded. — The Beginning of the End 245

XX.

THE SPIRIT OF SEVENTY-SIX.

The March to Dorchester. — Governor Shirley's. — Five Corners. — The Americans carry their Forts with them. — Rufus Putnam. — Consternation of the British. — The Fifth of March. — Washington in the Field. — The British must go. — St. Patrick's Day in the Morning 250

ILLUSTRATIONS.

	PAGE		PAGE
The Belles of Seventy-six . *Frontispiece*		Liberty Tree	66
Indian Wigwams	8	Gentleman of the Revolutionary	
Ancient Windmill	9	Day	69
Indian Execution	10	Old Hollis Street	71
Indian Sachem	13	A Tempest in a Big Tea-pot	73
The Puritans hang up their Hats	19	Old South	74
Old King's Chapel, Beacon Hill,		Broken Tea-chest	75
and Beacon	23	Revere's Picture of Boston in 1768	79
Old Corn Mill	23	The Heart and Crown	80
The Beacon	24	Three Doves	81
Old Curtis Homestead	25	The Blue Ball	82
Old Cocked Hat, Dock Square	26	"How shall I get through this	
Franklin's Birthplace	27	world?"	82
Helmets of the Puritan Time	28	Bunch of Grapes	83
Watchman	29	Franklin's Press	83
The Stocks and Whipping-post	36	The Province House	84
The Pillory	37	The Old Corner	88
Soldier of 1630	42	King's Chapel	90
Colony Flag	42	A Hackney Coach	91
Mutilating the Flag	43	Shirley Arms	91
The Old Sword	44	Old State House	93
Spinning-wheel	45	Speaker's Desk	94
Wool-wheel	46	Old Brick Church	94
Hand-loom	46	Trophies of Bennington	96
Pine-tree Shilling	47	Regimental Ensign taken at York-	
The Chimney-corner	48	town	99
Dinner-time	49	Sentry Go	100
Puritan Handwriting	51	The Great Elm	102
British Officer, 1688	54	The Great Mall, Haymarket, and	
The Boston Truck	61	Theatre in 1798	103
Chaise of 1775	63	Hancock Mansion	107
Equestrians, Revolutionary Period	64	British Lines on Boston Neck	111
Market Woman, 1775	65	The Guns "Hancock and Adams"	113

ILLUSTRATIONS.

	PAGE		PAGE
Brattle Street Church	119	American Siege Gun and Carriage	185
Cannon-ball in the Window	120	Hessian Flag	190
Faneuil Hall	121	Old Mile-stone	192
Lottery Ticket	122	Holden Chapel	195
New Faneuil Hall	125	Harvard Hall	197
Boston Stone	126	Massachusetts Hall	198
Green Dragon Tavern	129	The President's House	200
Sign of the Green Dragon	130	The Washington Elm, Cambridge	206
Christ Church	140	Early American Flag	208
Tomb of the Mathers	143	Washington's Headquarters	211
The Glasgow	144	Fort on Cobble Hill	212
The Old House in Ship (North) Street	150	Flag of Morgan's Rifles	213
		Flag of the Body-guard	217
Frankland's House	151	Lieutenant-Governor Oliver's	222
The Hutchinson Mansion	152	High Fort, Roxbury	231
Swords of Revolutionary Generals	156	The Parting Stone	232
Heights of Charlestown from the Navy Yard, 1826	165	Meeting-House Hill, Roxbury, 1790	233
Bunker Hill Monument	169	The Parsonage	234
Provincial Cartridge-box	174	Roxbury Fort, from a Powder-horn	237
Boston from Breed's Hill, 1791	179	The Warren Homestead	241
Relics from Warren's Body	183	Governor Shirley's Mansion	251

AROUND THE HUB.

I.

THE FIRST INHABITANTS.

ALL travellers agree that the way to see a country is to walk through it. You ride because the distance is long, or because you are in a hurry. But by walking you get the habit of observation. You learn to use your eyes. You are surprised to find common things growing interesting, or curious, or instructive. You see.

A traveller, who boasted of having visited many countries, got a friend to ask for him an introduction to the celebrated Humboldt. The gentleman at once called on the Baron.

"My friend," began the mediator, "claims to be a fellow-traveller. He, too, has been all over the world."

"Yes," replied the Baron, "and so has his trunk."

We will, at any rate, try not to imitate this traveller, whose trunk was considered quite as travelled as himself.

One thing more. Were we going to Rome, we should first "read up" a little, as we say, in order to gain such general knowledge as might serve us a good turn when we arrived in the Eternal City. What was learned in this way would be a great help in getting over the ground easily and quickly. Let us do this now. Let us take a long look back over the two hundred and fifty years uniting us with the time when our history is mute. Two centuries and a half! That does seem a long time. Yet, compared with the ages of which we know nothing, it is a mere fragment, a scrap, a tick of the clock.

The Indians, whose history we do not know, seem to have preferred living on the mainland. At any rate, the first white settlers in Boston Bay found none inhabiting the peninsula either of Shawmut or Mattapan, and a few only lived at Mishawum: these were the Indian names of Boston, Dorchester, and Charlestown.

INDIAN WIGWAMS.

But many skulls and human bones

were dug up on the eminence now called Pemberton Square,[1] in Boston, at a very early day, and the inhabitants believed them to be Indian remains.

These Indians mingled freely with the whites, showing a friendly disposition. Their numbers had been so greatly diminished by sickness that the well-armed English were

ANCIENT WINDMILL.

far too numerous to fear them as neighbors. But care was taken not to offend them. They came and went freely. They were amazed at the arts and implements of the white men. They never tired of looking on and seeing how dexterously these English carpenters handled

---

[1] Formerly Cotton Hill. It was so named from one of the earliest ministers of Boston, Rev. John Cotton, who lived there. Look in the biographical dictionaries for notices of this eminent divine.

their saws and wielded their axes. But they were not at all fond of work themselves. In fact, among the Indians, all the hard labor was performed by women. The men considered it degrading.

We are told that the first ship they saw was supposed to be a floating island, — the masts, trees; the sails, white clouds; the artillery, thunder and lightning. When they attempted to go to this island the cannon terrified them so that they fled into the woods.

"So big walk! So big speak! By and by kill!" they cried out in their terror.

The first windmill they saw beating the air with its long arms, they were afraid to approach. They believed the first ploughman turning the sod to be a wizard.

INDIAN EXECUTION.

The manners and customs of this people are very curious and very interesting, but we can only stop to relate one or two of their peculiarities.

They had laws which were strictly observed. If one of them committed a crime, or proved a coward in time of war, he was either driven from the tribe in disgrace, or, if the offence was too flagrant for this punishment, suffered death. In this case, the prisoner, securely bound, was led forth from the village, and dispatched by the stroke of a tomahawk.

Touching the care used to keep on good terms with the Indians, Governor Dudley[1] told this droll anecdote to a sea-captain who visited him.

One day, while a carpenter was cutting down a tree, and a crowd of Indians stood around, watching every blow with the greatest attention, the tree fell on one of them who did not get out of the way, killing him on the spot. The other Indians set up a great howling over the dead body, while the frightened carpenter ran and hid himself to escape their vengeance, for they foolishly thought him to blame for the death of their companion. The English tried to persuade them the carpenter was not at fault; but nothing short of his death would pacify them. They demanded that he should be given up to them for execution. Seeing them thus enraged, and fearing that they might fall upon and destroy them, in revenge, the English finally promised to hang the unlucky carpenter themselves. The Indians were told to come the next morning, and they would see him hanging from a particular tree. But the carpenter being a young and lusty fellow, and very useful, they concluded they could not spare him, and, there being in the fort an old bedridden weaver, who had

[1] For an account of Governor Joseph Dudley, consult the History of the Town of Roxbury.

not long to live, he was taken out to the tree and quietly hanged in the room of the carpenter, to the entire satisfaction of the Indians, who did not detect the cheat and who became good friends again.[1]

But in Butler's "Hudibras," you may read a story much like this in verse. Here it is: —

> "Our brethren of New England use
> Choice malefactors to excuse,
> And hang the guiltless in their stead;
> Of whom the churches have less need.
> As lately 't happened; in a town
> There liv'd a cobbler, and but one
> That out of doctrine could cut use,
> And mend men's lives as well as shoes.
> This precious brother having slain,
> In time of peace, an Indian,
> Not out of malice, but mere zeal,
> Because he was an infidel;
> The mighty Tottipottimoy
> Sent to our elders an envoy,
> Complaining sorely of the breach
> Of league, held forth by brother Patch,
> Against the articles in force
> Between both churches, his and ours;
> But they maturely having weigh'd
> They had no more but him o' th' trade,
> A man that serv'd them in a double
> Capacity to teach and cobble.

[1] This is in Captain N. Uring's "Voyages," a rare book. He was in Boston in 1709. A story similar to the versified one in Hudibras is told in Morton's "New English Canaan," thus making three independent sources to which it may be traced. Butler says it is a true story.

Resolv'd to spare him ; yet to do
The Indian Hoghan Moghan too
Impartial justice, in his stead did
Hang an old weaver that was bedrid."

This story may cause a laugh, but I do not see that it is either more improbable or more atrocious than the present practice in war of killing a certain number of innocent prisoners for the same number who may be executed by your enemy.

The head men among the Indians were called sachems, or sagamores. It may be interesting to jot down the names of a few of these Massachusetts sagamores, — Obquamhud, Canacocome, Obbatinewat, Nattawahunt, Cawkatant, Chikatabut, Quadaquina, Huttamoiden, Apannow.

One more anecdote will serve to illustrate the cuteness of the Indians.

A gentleman who wished to make a present of oranges to a lady, sent them with a letter by his

INDIAN SACHEM.

Indian servant. The letter told how many were sent. On the way the fragrant smell of the fruit proved too great a temptation for the Indian boy. His mouth fairly watered for a taste, but having seen his master read and write letters, he was possessed with the idea that the paper he carried would tell of him if he touched the oranges. He therefore put the letter carefully under a stone, and then, going off to a distance, ate several oranges, feeling perfectly safe. When he came to deliver the remainder of the oranges the lady saw by the letter that some were missing. She charged the Indian with the theft, but he for some time stoutly denied it, and asserted that the letter lied; nor was it until threatened with punishment that he confessed, so certain was he that he had put the letter where it could not see him.

This anecdote shows that the Indians were no fools. Their civilization, as we term it, only began with the coming of the white people, but they were far from being an inferior race, like the Esquimaux, the Patagonians, or the Digger Indians of California. They lived in rude, conical huts of bark, called wigwams. They went almost naked, even in winter. They lived by fishing and hunting; and although their tools to build themselves canoes, their spears to take fish, and their arrows to kill game were all made of stone, they were very expert indeed in the use of them. We can now see these things carefully preserved in the cabinets of our museums, and the skill with which they are made excites our wonder.[1]

The Indians believed in a god of evil, as well as of good, to whom they ascribed all their calamities, such as death, pestilence, or famine. To this evil spirit, therefore, they prayed that he would cease from hurting them. Their great and good spirit, or Manitou, was the god of peace, plenty, and happiness. To him they prayed for a continuance of these blessings. But they most feared, and perhaps prayed oftenest to, the evil spirit, or devil.

They made offerings to their gods the same as other ancient peoples, — the Greeks, for instance. They believed the earth had been formed of a grain of sand. Their heaven was beyond the highest mountain-peaks, which they dared not ascend for fear of offending the god who dwelt among them. And what is more curious still, they had a tradition of the deluge which had drowned all the inhabitants of earth, except one powaw and his wife, who escaped by climbing to the top of the White Mountains. When the waters subsided they descended again to earth, and from them came all subsequent peoples.

The Indians possessed many virtues which, uncivilized as they were, made them superior in some things to the more civilized Pale-faces. For example, they were extremely hospitable. The weary stranger was considered

[1] Go to the Museum of Natural History and look at the stone pestles, axes, arrow-heads, etc.

the guest of the whole village into which he had strayed.
All vied with each other in showing him kindness. If
hungry, they fed him; if cold, they warmed him; and the
next day they guided him on his journey, — and all without reward.

But English hospitality was a puzzle to them. So one
of them asked an Englishman to explain it. "If I go
into a white man's house," he said, "and ask for victuals
and drink, they say, 'Where is your money?' And if I
have none they say, 'Get out, you Indian dog!'"

In common civility, and in what are called "good manners," these untutored beings could often give their white
neighbors a lesson. Did an Indian come into a town he
would either be surrounded or followed by a gaping crowd.
All this made him feel very ill at ease. He considered it
great rudeness. When a stranger came into an Indian
village no one intruded upon him. He was allowed to go
on his way without interruption. The Indians satisfied
their curiosity by watching him from a distance.

Upon the death of a warrior of the tribe, he was buried
in a sitting posture; and his pipe and tomahawk, with
any trinket he may have possessed, were placed near him.
For even the savage believed in a resurrection; though
heaven was to him a land of plenty, abounding in game,
which he would again hunt in his own proper form. So
his weapons were placed where he could grasp them.

The Indians were very grave, attentive, and courteous.

Even if they did not believe or could not understand a thing, they took care not to let it be seen. One of our ministers having explained to them the history of the Christian religion, — the fall of our first parents by eating an apple, the coming of Christ, his miracles, and sufferings, — an Indian orator stood up to thank him.

"What you have told us," he began, "is all very good. It is indeed bad to eat apples; it is better to make them all into cider."

He then told the missionary, in his turn, an ancient tradition, handed down through many generations of his people, how two starving hunters, having killed a deer, were about to satisfy their hunger when they saw a beautiful young woman descend out of the clouds and stand beside them. They were at first afraid, but taking courage offered the spirit the choicest portion of their meat. She tasted it, and then, telling them to return in thirteen moons to the same spot, vanished. They returned, as she bade them, at the appointed time. Where the good spirit had touched the ground with her right hand they found maize; with her left, beans; and where she stood was the luxuriant tobacco-plant.

The missionary plainly showed his disgust and disbelief in this idle tale, saying to the Indian, "What I delivered to you were sacred truths; but what you tell me is mere fable, fiction, and falsehood."

The offended Indian gravely replied:

"My brother, it seems your friends have not well instructed you in the rules of common civility. You saw that we, who understand and practise these rules, believed all your stories: why do you refuse to believe ours?"

But we must now take leave of these original inhabitants of Boston. They have all long since gone to their Happy Hunting Grounds, beyond the Great White Mountains. By and by, except for our books, their very existence would be doubted. Providence or destiny has swept them from the land where their fathers dwelt. By and by, seeing a strange figure upon the great seal of the State, some youth will ask his father:—

"What is that outlandish-looking being?"

"That? Oh, that is an Indian."

"Is it a man?"

"Certainly, it is a man."

"Where is he?"

"God knows, my son."

"Where does he live; where is his country?"

"He has no country."

"But why, then, is he on the seal?"

"Ah! It was put there when he was strong, and we weak. This broad land was once his. We took it from him. The seal is now the only thing we have to remember him by."

II.

THE PURITANS HANG UP THEIR HATS.

THE English people who came with Governor Winthrop first located upon the peninsula of Mishawum, which they called Charlestown, probably in honor of Charles I., their sovereign.[1] They found here a single white man named Thomas Walford, living very peaceably and contentedly among the Indians. They also discovered that the peninsula of Shawmut had one solitary white inhabitant whose name was William Blackstone. They could see every day the smoke curling above this man's lonely cabin. He, too, was a Puritan clergyman, like many of those who had now come to make a home in the New World, free from the tyranny of the English bishops. Still another Englishman, Samuel Maverick by name, had

---

[1] I say "probably" because the river Charles had previously received this name from Captain John Smith in honor of the same prince. It was the first town here to receive an English name after Plymouth.

built a house, and with the help of David Thompson, a fort which mounted four small cannon, truly called "murtherers," and was living very comfortably on the island that is now East Boston. And again, by looking across the bay, to the south, the smoke of an English cottage, on Thompson's Island, was probably seen stealing upward to the sky. So that we certainly know these people were the first settlers of Boston.[1]

But scarcity of water, and sickness, which soon broke out among them, made the settlers at Charlestown very discontented. They began to scatter. Indeed, this peninsula was too small properly to accommodate all of them with their cattle. Therefore good William Blackstone, with true hospitality, came in their distress to tell them there was a fine spring of pure water at Shawmut, and to invite them there. Probably his account induced quite a number to remove at once; while others, wishing to make farms, looked out homes along the shores of the mainland, at Medford, Newtown (Cambridge), Watertown, and Roxbury. A separate company of colonists also settled at Mattapan, or Dorchester. The dissatisfaction with Charles-

[1] These may be the same persons we see referred to by the new comers as "old planters." But six years before the arrival of Winthrop's company, quite a small colony had begun settlement at Nantasket (Hull). Among them were Roger Conant, John Lyford, and John Oldham, all conspicuous in the early annals of Plymouth and Massachusetts. Plymouth lays a tax on this little plantation of "Natascot" in 1628, and Mrs. Thompson, at Squantum, and Mr. Blackstone are also taxed.

Although the chief men of the colony continued for some time yet to favor the plan of a fortified town farther inland, Boston had now become too firmly rooted, and the people too unwilling, to make a second change of location practicable, or even desirable. So this project was abandoned, though not before high words passed between Winthrop and Dudley about it. The governor then removed the frame of his new house from Cambridge, or Newtown, to Boston, setting it up on the land between Milk Street, Spring Lane, and Washington Street. One of the finest springs being upon his lot, the name Spring Lane is easily traced. The people first located themselves within the space now comprised between Milk, Bromfield, Tremont, and Hanover Streets, and the water, or, in general terms, upon the southeasterly slope of Beacon Hill. Pemberton Hill soon became a favorite locality. The North End, including that portion of the town north of Union Street, was soon built up by the new emigrants coming in, or by removals from the South End, as all the town south of this district was called. In time a third district on the north side of Beacon Hill grew up, and was called the West End. And in the old city these general divisions continue to-day.

Shawmut, we remember, was the first name Boston had. Now the settlers at Charlestown, seeing always before them a high hill topped with three little peaks, had already, and very aptly too, we think, named Shawmut

THE PURITANS HANG UP THEIR HATS. 23

Trimountain.[1] But when they began to remove there they called it Boston, after a place of that name in England, and because they had determined beforehand to give to their chief town this name. So says the second highest person among them, Deputy Governor Thomas Dudley.

The settlers built their first church on the ground now covered by Brazer's Building, in State Street. It is a pity that no picture has handed down to us the appearance of this primitive edifice, in which Wilson and Cotton preached, and Winthrop and Vane went to meeting. Directly in front of the meeting-house was the town market-place. Where Quincy Market is was the principal landing-place. The Common was set apart as a pasture-ground and training-field. A ferry was established be-

OLD KING'S CHAPEL, BEACON HILL, AND BEACON.

OLD CORN MILL.

---

[1] The location of old "Treamount," now Tremont Street, around the base of the three-peaked hill, at a very early day, confirms this view of the name Trimountain.

tween Boston and Charlestown; a rude battery was erected upon Castle Island; a wind-mill, to grind corn, upon the hill at the north end of the town. A beacon was set up on the summit of Trimountain, and a fort upon the southernmost hill of the town. From this time these hills took the names of Windmill, Beacon, and Fort Hills. The last has now wholly disappeared, having been dug down some years since; and the first very soon changed its name to Copp's Hill.

The fort on the island was designed to defend the town from attack by sea, the beacon to give notice to the neighboring towns of the approach of an enemy. If by day, a flag hoisted upon it was the signal; if by night, a fire lighted in an iron cage at the top, filled with pitch and light wood, could be seen from a great distance. In either case, the country people were to take their arms and repair to the town as fast as possible.

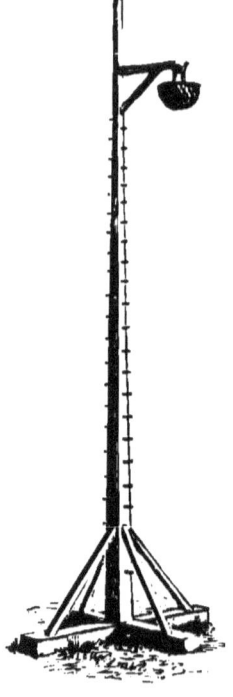

THE BEACON.

Having thus seen Boston settled and equipped for defence, let us now inquire a little how the people lived, and what manner of folk they were.

The first houses were naturally very poor and humble

dwellings. They were hurriedly put together for immediate shelter. It is believed some of the poorer sort of people lived for a time in wigwams, which the Indians taught them how to build. Some of the were roofed with a thatch of rushes for a roof. Instead of chimneys, they built oaken cribwise ... smearing them inside and out with clay. And ...

OLD CURTIS HOMESTEAD.

wood, and probably few if any had more than one story. The old Curtis Homestead, near Boylston Station, in Roxbury, is a good specimen of these early houses. And what makes this house remarkable is that it has always been occupied by the Curtis family. We judge that the best house in all these plantations, as they were called, was the one built at Roxbury by Governor Dudley, because

Winthrop scolded him sharply for having a wainscot of claphoards inside, and some little tasteful ornament outside, as setting an example of pride and extravagance.

Houses with gables, like the old Cocked Hat in Dock Square, and houses with the upper story projecting, like Franklin's birthplace, were built very early; but this jutting upper story was not intended, as some people believe, to enable the inmates to fire down upon the heads of imaginary assailants, or to scald them with boiling water. Far from it. They were simply the kind of houses these people had been used to live in in Old England. Such chimneys as were then built are a wonder to our generation! They seem more like towers than chimneys. A few specimens of the early architecture may still be seen in North, Charter, and Salem Streets.

OLD COCKED HAT, DOCK SQUARE.

As soon as possible the inhabitants of Boston enclosed two large fields, called the Fort Field and the Mill Field, in which their cows, goats, swine, and sheep were folded, under the charge of a keeper.

Unfortunately the streets were from the first very crooked indeed. They seem to have succeeded the foot-paths, which, of course, took the easiest way over or among the hills, without regard to whether it was, or was not, the nearest. Modern Boston has spent millions trying to remedy this want of forecast, but her ways are still crooked, and crooked they must remain.

FRANKLIN'S BIRTHPLACE.

The government of town affairs was managed by citizens, especially appointed for the purpose, called selectmen; and this same form of town government is still in force throughout New England. So the Puritans deserve credit for establishing a good and durable system for small communities.

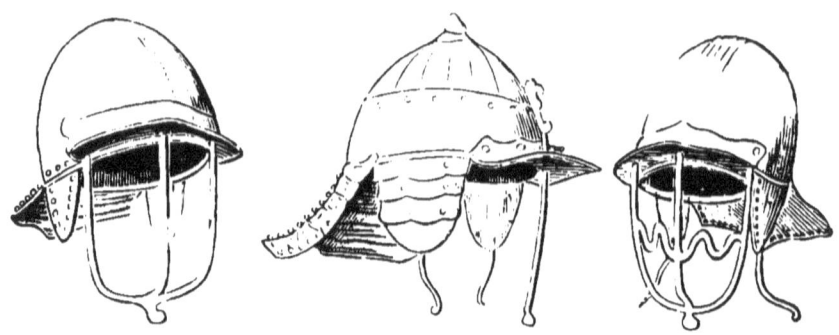

HELMETS OF THE PURITAN TIME.

III.

OLD BOSTON NOTIONS.

BEFORE there were any bells in the town, a drum was beat at the curfew to warn the people that it was bed-time, and to put out their lights. It was also the usual signal for the train-bands to get under arms; the drummer, who was regularly chosen for the purpose, marching around the town, beating lustily the while. The drummers and fifers of the Ancient and Honorable Artillery Company still keep up this old custom. The martial roll of a drum was certainly a startling and a singular call to meeting on the peaceful Sabbath, but it was so used, the same as in a camp.

Some of the rules for keeping order now seem very strict, some seem laughable. A town-watch was organized, which went about the streets crying the hour. Thus, in the stillness of night, they would bawl out in a loud singsong at some corner, "Twelve o'clock, and all's well!" A citizen, whose sleep was disturbed by these outcries, inquired if it would not be better for the watch to cry out when all was not well, and to let well enough alone.

Imagine eight stout watchmen, in their great watch-coats, with staves and lanterns, and walking two and two, each night perambulating every hole and corner of the town. Lads could not then sit up late with their sweethearts, for, if the watch saw lights twinkling after ten o'clock, they were required to knock at the door and demand the reason. If the watch saw young men and maidens taking a walk together after dark, they could send them home in a hurry to their lodgings, or put them under lock and key till morning. They could order dancing and singing in a private or public house to be stopped. And they visited the taverns or ordinaries, as they were called, and made the landlord shut up his house and turn his noisy guests into the street. Nowadays we should hardly submit to such things, but they were then thought to be right and proper to the good order and decorum of society.

WATCHMAN.

About these taverns. The Puritans certainly hit upon a droll way of preventing drunkenness. They licensed taverns, and they licensed the sale of liquor. Yes, and they made a law fixing the price of a morning dram, too, so that the tavern-keeper could be fined for refusing to sell what the law allowed. So we see they were not total abstainers by any means. But this is the way they stopped drunkenness. If a stranger went into a tavern and called for liquor, a constable followed him in and stationed himself at his elbow. When the constable thought the stranger had drank enough, if he asked for more, the officer said, "No, friend, you can't have it." And not another drop could he get.

But for a long time the town, at night, was wrapped in darkness. As soon as it was dark the citizens went to bed. No other lights shone out of doors except the moon or the stars. So not many would venture into the streets unless there by necessity, — such as sickness, or death, or a fire. There were no pavements, and no sidewalks. These conveniences had to wait until the town grew rich enough to afford them. The people, or some of them, had, it is true, been accustomed to such things in the old country; many had lived there in luxury and ease; but here they had first to get over their hard struggle to obtain a bare living; and luxuries, of course, were not to be thought of.

When these people met, they did not call each other

Mister and Missis, as we now do, but "Master" and "Mistress,"[1] if they were above the rank of farmer, mechanic, or laborer; and "Goodman" and "Goodwife" if they belonged to either of these classes.

They did not believe in social equality at all. Society was divided into distinct classes, the same as in England, and each class insisted upon the distinction that belonged to it. Thus, only a man or woman of birth, or holding a place in the highest rank of society, was a gentleman or a gentlewoman. The terms were then applied to persons of gentle birth or breeding, and not to manners, as is the case to-day. We find in old records the abbreviation "Gent." written only after the names of those entitled to it by this old custom. And the custom was long scrupulously preserved. Those who were husbandmen, or weavers, or carpenters, had their occupation always set down after the name.

In those days a governor, a colonel, a judge, or a minister must be addressed by his title always, or it would be considered ill breeding. We must remember it was the day of kings and nobles, lords and ladies, and that these colonists were only Englishmen transplanted. They did not come over the sea to found a republic of equality, but a new England.

[1] The word "Dame" was also used, generally when speaking of the head of a household; and in the case of gentle lineage, it was "Lady So and So."

Besides these classes were the family servants, male and female, whom everybody looked down upon, and who performed menial labor of every kind. These were generally poor people who wished to emigrate, but not having the means so to do, bound or sold themselves for one, two, or more years, to pay the expenses of their outfit and passage.

So we see, at the top of society, the gentleman and lady; in the middle walk, the goodman and goodwife; while the common laborer, if a freeman, still looked down a little upon the bond-servant.

By and by negroes were brought to Boston and sold and held as slaves; and this state of things continued until after the Revolutionary War. Then, again, a shipload of prisoners of war would be sent over from England, and sold for a term of service to such as were in want of laborers or farm-hands. All this sounds very strange to us, but it is nevertheless all true.

The people were called to meeting on the Sabbath, as we have said, by the drum, and to occasions of public ceremony by sounding a trumpet loudly through the town. This ancient custom belonged to the days of chivalry, and no proclamation was held to be properly published without it. The trumpeter was an officer something like the modern town-crier, who, not many years ago, went through the streets ringing a bell, and, when a crowd had collected, shouting with stentorian lungs a lost child, a political meeting, or a public auction.

Except for sickness, or for actual infirmity, no one was allowed to stay away from meeting. And if any one spoke disrespectfully of the minister, or used an oath, he could, on complaint, be fined. An officer, called a beadle, was appointed to go about the town and pick up all those "stragglers" who were loitering there on the Sabbath. If they could not give a good excuse, they were fined for not attending divine worship. These same officers, afterwards called tithingmen, carried long wands, with which they rapped smartly over the bare poll any one who fell asleep in meeting during the sermon, and in the same way they kept unruly boys in order. As soon as a drowsy citizen was seen to nod, down came the staff with a loud thwack on his bald pate. Men and women did not then sit together as they now do, but each occupied a different side of the house. It was not considered seemly for the sexes to mingle in public. As the sermons were always long, the tithingmen were no doubt kept busy. On the sacred desk an hour-glass marked the slow progress of time.

For a long time neither organ nor instrumental music of any kind was allowed in a Puritan meeting-house. The people believed such things sinful. They stood up in their places and sang the old psalms, which could hardly now be sung with sober faces by any church choir in Boston. The psalm was "lined out" (a line read at a time) by the deacon, and then repeated by the congregation.

The Sabbath was above all to be kept holy. It began at the sunset hour on Saturday and continued until the same time on Sunday. All work ceased. No one was permitted to travel on this day except in a case of absolute necessity. If a traveller could not reach his destination by sunset of Saturday, he must go no farther than the first house where he could obtain accommodation. Any one violating the Sabbath by travelling, or being upon public highways, except as just stated, was liable to a fine. Such is the law of Massachusetts to-day. Every railway train or other public conveyance running upon the Sabbath breaks this old law.

The strictness with which the Sabbath was kept by our Puritan ancestors caused a joke now and then at their expense. It was said that some of the old women would not brew Saturdays because the beer would, in course, work on the Lord's Day following.

In common affairs the people made use of Scripture terms. They called each other "brother" and "sister." And really about all the law they had was derived from Scripture (the Judaic Law), until the want of written law became an evil so great that they were compelled to establish a code called the "Body of Libertys," which was by general consent alone obeyed. The reason of this long neglect was that, some of their customs being in conflict with the laws of England, they were afraid to put them in writing. But to make such customs operate as laws was equally a violation of the privileges given them by the king in their charter. And the king gave and the king could take away their charter; and he finally did take it away.

Still, these were, on the whole, a sober, industrious, and God-fearing people. The custom of drinking malt or spirituous liquors was general, but drunkenness was considered disgraceful, and was punished, sometimes by making the culprit wear the letter "D" (for drunkard) in scarlet, sewed on over white cloth, upon his breast. Idleness was also punished; so were lying, cheating, scolding, and other offences which the law does not now reach at all. For these minor misdeeds they had the stocks, the pillory, and the whipping-post; for great crimes they had the scaffold.

The stocks, pillory, and whipping-post were usually placed in front of the meeting-house, which was commonly the town-house and court-house as well. In Boston these terrors to evil-doers were for a long time located in King, now State Street. People ran to see punishment inflicted by the lash, or to stare at some miserable creature sitting in the stocks, or standing upright in the pillory, as they would at any other show.

Within the century the public whipping-post, appropriately painted a blood-red, continued to afford its disgusting spectacle of daily punishment to the mob, whose coarse jeers and shouts frequently drowned the screams of the victims. The scholars of one of the public schools could look directly down from their windows upon such scenes as

THE STOCKS AND WHIPPING-POST.

this. Thanks to a more enlightened sentiment, they are now spared such revolting sights.

"Here women were taken from a huge cage, in which

they were dragged on wheels from prison, and tied to the post with bare backs, on which thirty or forty lashes were bestowed. . . . A little farther on in the street was to be seen the pillory, with three or four fellows fastened by the head and hands, and standing for an hour in that helpless posture, exposed to gross and cruel insult from the multitude, who pelted them incessantly with rotten eggs and every repulsive kind of garbage that could be collected."[1]

THE PILLORY.

The place of public execution was our beautiful Common, which had been from the first set apart as a common pasture-ground and training-field for all the inhabitants of the town. Several Quakers suffered the death-penalty here for their faith, and were buried beneath its green sod. During the British armed occupation the Common also witnessed military executions; and at least one poor fellow was shot near the foot of the Common, by a file of his comrades, for deserting the Continental colors. Pirates have also been hung on this spot. All these victims lie in unknown graves.[2]

---

[1] Recollections of Samuel Breck, pp. 36, 37.
[2] The public gibbet was afterwards erected on the Neck, at the entrance to the town.

In the early days of the colony the authority of a father over his children was almost as absolute as it was among the ancient Romans. Until a son or a daughter was of age the will of a parent was law. Children treated their parents with the greatest respect, and their elders with studied deference. It was considered forward in them to speak to an older person unless first spoken to. Neither a son nor a daughter would have dared to contract an engagement of marriage without the knowledge and consent of his or her own parents. We do not say such things may not have happened. Human nature was the same then as now, and love laughed at obstacles; but in every way the letter and spirit of the law strongly upheld and assisted the parental authority, according to Scripture ideas. It is true a father could not sacrifice his son, like Abraham, but his word was law; and disobedience was punishable the same as other offences.[1]

We find such games as foot-ball, stool-ball, and quoits permitted, though not in the streets. Therefore the young were not wholly without out-of-door sports. But the Puritans abominated dancing, and they regarded dancing round a May-Pole as so little short of idolatrous that they cut one down that had been erected by some jovial spirits near Boston. Stage-plays and instrumental music they

[1] The selectmen had authority under the colony to order parents to bind their children as apprentices, or put them out to service; and, in case of refusal, the town took the children from the charge of the parents.

abhorred. The possession of cards or dice by a family would have brought down upon the owner sharp reproof from his minister, as introducing the works of Satan himself into the community.

No strangers were permitted to live within the town, without giving bonds to save the town harmless from all charge for taking care of them.[1] Entertaining foreigners, or receiving "inmates, servants, or journeymen coming for help, in physic or surgery without leave of the selectmen," was twenty shillings a week fine. Thus we see these people admitted that almost every act and deed should be open to public scrutiny. Domiciliary visits have always been classed among the most arbitrary acts of a government; saying who a citizen shall or shall not receive into his house, as his guest, as an invasion of private rights. But these things were submitted to with good grace, although strangers sometimes fared badly in Puritan Boston, unless they chanced to have letters or friends vouching for their religious opinions.[2]

Education was not neglected. Nothing is more credit-

[1] This is quaint. "Also this day (1638), Richard Tuttell, our brother, hath undertaken for one Dorothie Bill, a widdowe, a sojourner in his house, to discharge the Toune of any charge that may befall the Toune for anything about her."

[2] And this is pointed. "Imprymis: It is agreed that noe further allotments shalbe graunted unto any new comers, but such as may be likely to be received members of the congregation." Nor were inhabitants allowed to sell houses or lands without consent of the town authorities; or even to become inhabitants without such leave.

able to these Bostonians than one of their earliest recorded acts entreating Brother Philemon Pormont to become their schoolmaster. And not long afterwards Daniel Maude is mentioned as being the town pedagogue.

Signs, omens, and portents were most religiously believed in. If a person was charged with murder, he or she was made to touch the face of the dead under the belief that if guilty the fresh blood would gush forth from the wound. This cruel test was applied to Mary Martin. It is said the blood flowed forth, and she then confessed her crime. Sorcery, witchcraft, the power of malignant touch and sight, were also implicitly believed in;[1] but they also were everywhere in Christendom. So the people of New England, superstitious as they were, were not more so than the rest of the civilized globe.

Religious toleration had no place in ancient Boston. Only members of the congregation were eligible to the rights of freemen. No other could hold any office or give his vote in town affairs. Those who held aloof were considered proper objects of suspicion. Episcopalians were given the cold shoulder, although their faith was that of the realm of England. But Quakers and Baptists were scourged, banished, and imprisoned; and some of the former, as we have related, were even hanged. The Puri-

[1] Refer to your Encyclopædia under the article "King's Evil." The other forms of superstition are too well established to require an authority to be given. The stories told in the old chronicles almost surpass belief.

tans pleaded the law of self-preservation for inflicting the death-penalty. The Quakers pleaded the higher law of conscience for coming half way to meet it.[1]

Fasts and Thanksgivings were early introduced as special occasions occurred. There is probably no reason for observing the particular day now set apart as Thanksgiving Day. The first public fast was ordered to be kept February 5, 1631, in consequence of the distress the Boston colonists were in for want of food, but a ship having arrived with provisions, the day was changed to one of thanksgiving.

Train-bands were quickly formed in the colony. Steel caps, or helmets, corselets, or breast and back-piece, gorgets, and possibly other defensive armor, were worn. Usually a quilted tunic of undressed leather, called a buff-coat, and arrow-proof, was worn underneath the cuirass. The arms were the snapchance (a firelock), the matchlock (a musket fired by applying a match to the touch-hole), pike, halberd, curtal-axe, and sword. Carbines and pistols were also in use. Swords were only worn on occasions of ceremony, or by military officers when on duty, and not as part of a gentleman's dress.

Speaking of military customs, we are told that on general training-days, when all the train-bands repaired to the Common, it was the practice for each captain to offer up a prayer before beginning to exercise his men.

[1] See the Poet Whittier's "The King's Missive," which is true to history.

Some of the sterner sort of Puritans hated the cross so much that they could not even endure the sight of it on  the flag of England, their flag. The sign of the cross, made by the ministers when performing the rite of baptism, was one of their grounds of complaint with the Church of England. They considered it a ceremony of the Church of Rome, which they detested. Consequently, one day, in a fit of anger, or religious zeal, or both, John Endicott cut the cross out of the flag with his dagger.

SOLDIER OF 1630.

The more sober and moderate people were badly frightened at this bold deed, which was in reality little, if anything, short of treasonable. But for some time afterward no flag at all was hoisted over the Castle. Indeed, it was seriously talked over whether a new flag should be adopted, or the old one restored. A singular compromise, however, prevailed. The colony troops were permitted to carry colors without the cross; while, to save appearances,

COLONY FLAG.

the old flag was again hoisted over the castle walls. The headstrong Endicott was censured, and disqualified from holding office for a year. Perhaps this, too, was a blind.

Thus, within a few years after colonizing New England, these people refused to give up their charter when required to do so by the king; they made laws conflicting with the laws of England; they suspended the use of the national flag; and presently they coined money, like any independent state. None of these things passed unnoticed; but the civil wars in England postponed the day of reckoning some time longer. The reigning monarchs of the House of Stuart had their hands full at home.

MUTILATING THE FLAG.

Among the Puritan settlers the common method of voting was the old Athenian way of holding up the hand. Voting by the voice, "Aye," or "No," and voting by ballot, were also practised. No names were written on the paper ballot. The affirmative votes had some private mark by which the voter could identify it; the negative ones were left blank. The voters passed through a room where the magistrates were sitting, dropped their votes into a hat, and passed out; while electioneering went on outside pretty much as it does to-day.

Some of the governors assumed considerable parade. Winthrop and Vane were seldom seen abroad unattended by a guard of halberdiers or musketeers. Some little state was considered due to the office, some to the man.

Simplicity of dress prevailed among the people. The wearing of costly apparel, such as gold and silver lace, points, embroidered girdles, slashed sleeves, and large ruffs, was expressly forbidden. Still it was not wholly abolished; for the old portraits of the time show that neither men nor women were at all averse to being painted in their finery; and there are instances where people who were complained of for displaying some of these forbidden things in public, were excused upon proving that they could afford such expense.

THE OLD SWORD.

The high, steeple-crowned hat, a doublet, or tunic, of some dark color, confined at the waist by a belt, loose trunks or trousers, reaching to the knee and tied, stockings of silk or wool, coming up to the knee, with stout shoes, was the usual attire of the men; a broad, falling collar, stiff with starch, completed the dress, and frequently a short cloak was worn out of doors.

Women wore hats similar to those worn by men, gowns of woollen stuff, and high-heeled shoes with peaked toes. They sometimes, for full dress, wore the slip, or petticoat, and the overdress, now so fashionable. Capes, collars, and cuffs were also used at the pleasure of the wearer. It was thought a very immodest act to expose the neck or arms bare. Ornaments for the person, or jewelry, except rings, were very rarely seen.

Marriages were not solemnized by the clergy, but by the magistrates. The service was very simple indeed. No Puritan maiden would have plighted her troth with a ring for the world. Funerals were conducted with as little pomp as possible. The mourners followed the bier to the grave, stood around until it was filled up, and then dispersed.

Nearly every family made its own cloth, or at least the yarn for the weaver's use. The spinning-

SPINNING-WHEEL.

wheel for cotton, flax, and wool was found in every house, and was seldom idle. Habits of industry and economy

WOOL-WHEEL.

were sedulously instilled into old and young. So while women spun, men and boys toiled in the fields. It was a continued struggle with a rigorous climate and unfertile soil that made them count the cost of everything beforehand. "As empty as a New English purse," was a common saying. "We cannot live by our hands in this country," says Nat Ward.[1]

For a long time silver and gold coins were very scarce,— so scarce that wampum, brass farthings, and even musket-bullets, were made lawful money. Commodities were exchanged at fixed values, instead of money. But by and by the colonists grew bold. They usurped the right of the crown to coin money, and made it themselves from silver

HAND-LOOM.

bullion. King Charles II. was very angry when he heard of it, but was graciously pacified, it is said, upon being told that the tree embossed on the pieces of silver was

[1] Called the Simple Cobbler. Look him up.

the oak in which his Majesty hid himself when he was a hunted fugitive, flying from the troops of the Parliament. A good impression of one of the Pine Tree Shillings of the time is now worth twenty dollars, — about one hundred times its original value.

PINE-TREE SHILLING.

A great many articles of domestic use, such as kitchen utensils, furniture, table-ware, etc., may be seen among the collections preserved in the Old South. Antique arms, portraits, etc., are also carefully treasured here, and in the cabinets of the Massachusetts Historical, and the New England Historic Genealogical Societies.

Stoves being unknown, a huge cavern of a fireplace, with a brick-oven, sometimes large enough to conceal a whole family, performed the family cooking. Into one side an iron crane was firmly driven, on which the pot simmered and the kettle sung, while the cat purred in a snug corner. Andirons supported the blazing logs which snapped and spit and hissed, while the joint of meat, with a long iron prong, called a spit, thrust through it, was emitting a most savory odor. From time to time, the spit had to be turned so that the meat might not be scorched or underdone. While this was going on, the cook raked out from the hot embers, and dropped into her apron, a dozen or so of fine, plump, and mealy potatoes, roasted to a "T"; or perhaps it was a red herring. All being ready, she went to the door, and putting the tin dinner-horn to her lips, gave the welcome summons to the noonday meal.

THE CHIMNEY CORNER.

The family sat down around a table, seldom covered with a cloth, and furnished only with pewter plates and platters, spoons, and mugs instead of china. Sometimes there was a little silver, but not often; sometimes a little Holland delft, but more commonly none at all. Earthenware was generally used, and very soon manufactured by the colonists themselves. Beer or cider would be on the table, if it was in the cellar. All being seated, the head of the family, giving a preliminary cough, and casting his eye around the board to see that the young ones' faces were of proper length, said grace.

Sometimes this grace was so long that the younger members of the family grew nervous and fidgety, especially if they were very hungry. It is related that Ben. Franklin,

DINNER TIME.

when a lad, once asked his father why he did n't say grace over the whole barrel of beef or pork, instead of over each piece and every day. We can imagine the look old Josias Franklin gave him for his question.

A great deal of the early furniture was brought over from England, and is now highly prized. The high-backed chairs, chests of drawers, cradles, tables, tall bedsteads, etc., were often quaintly carved, and were very strongly made. Pewter or brass candlesticks, sconces (branched candlesticks that could be fixed to the wall), lighted the good people about the house, or to bed. All these articles, if in good condition, now bring fabulous prices. Indeed, a great deal of our modern furniture is patterned after them. So you see that old things are not without value, and that like the magician in the story, we are willing to exchange new lamps for old. But how the Puritans would have stared at the bare idea!

Carpets were not used. The floors were kept well scrubbed, and, in the common rooms, well sanded. A rug or two was no uncommon thing. But the master of every house had his sword, and his Bible, with which he was equally familiar.

I have now shown you a very simple and patriarchal community. Neither social, political, or religious equality had a place in it. I do not try to make you think them perfect, but to represent the Puritan founders of Boston as they actually were. Only great courage and fortitude could have carried them safely through all their trials. Their history is so interesting, and their deeds are so remarkable, and of such widespread influence, that no city of the world, Rome perhaps excepted, has had so much written about it. That interest will never grow less; for this handful of exiles really founded not merely a New

England, but an empire greater than they could ever have imagined; and the world will always hold them in great respect for the success they achieved. But, after all, the Dutch founded the great city of this continent. They had, it would seem, the better geographical knowledge.

PURITAN HANDWRITING.

IV.

FORT HILL, AN INTERLUDE.

NOW that we know what sort of people our New England ancestors were, let us again, after a lapse of fifty-six years, look in upon them and note the kind of social and political destiny they have worked out for themselves.

By this time nearly all of the original settlers have died. A mere handful of white-haired men remain, who were themselves lads in their teens when the colonists lighted their first camp-fires at Mishawum. But as a little leaven leavens the whole lump, so the Puritan idea surviving in these men keeps alive the spirit of the fathers. That idea is virtual independence, both in Church and State.

That idea, smouldering under the ashes of outward loyalty, has led to acts which have roused the ire of King Charles II., and he, in right kingly wrath, has taken away the ancient charter which the colonists received from his royal father's hands. With one stroke of the royal pen all the great privileges they have hitherto enjoyed are swept away.

But King Charles is dead. His brother, the Duke of York, ascends the throne as James II. Charles was a bad man, but James is a bad king.

Our Bostonians submit with very ill grace to their change of condition; but there is no help for it. The new monarch is proclaimed at the town-house with sorrowful and affected pomp, in presence of the eight military companies, and with volleys of musketry and of cannon. The people then disperse to nurse the wrath they dare not openly show.

By and by Sir Edmund Andros, the king's governor, comes with a battalion of royal troops and a frigate. Tyranny is to be backed up by force. For the first time the colonists feel the power they have provoked.

The frigate anchors in the stream, with its guns covering the town. The troops are quartered in Gibbs' elegant stone dwelling on Fort Hill.[1] From the very day in which he sets foot within the town, Sir Edmund begins to grind and oppress the people. In a short time he establishes a despotism as intolerable as that of his master in England. From dislike the people advance to hatred.

---

[1] As these were the first regular soldiers ever seen in Boston, they were objects of great curiosity. They carried guns with a short lance fixed in the muzzle. It was, more properly, a dagger. This was the first form of the bayonet. It had to be removed in firing; and, as this proved very awkward in action, the French succeeded in fixing the weapon to the muzzle, so that the gun could be discharged with it on. The sabre-bayonet is only a modification of the old original bayonet.

While Andros is thus sowing with free hand the seeds of rebellion, news is suddenly brought by a vessel of the landing of the Prince of Orange, and that all England is in revolt. This news is the match to the powder. Sir Edmund has been living in the magazine. His government vanishes in the explosion.

BRITISH OFFICER.
1688.

Fort Hill, where the king's troops are, is one of the pleasantest eminences with which nature adorns the town. If it should ever pass into a byword, then, indeed, will a glorious event cease to have its monument.[1] The fortress stands on the brow of the hill, with a battery lower down, next the water. It is strongly built of timber and earth, and mounts heavy cannon. It flies the royal standard. It is now the castle of tyranny.

The foot-way leading to the battery is called the Bat-

---

[1] No place in Boston seems more appropriate for a commemorative monument than this. A portion of the wall of the lower battery, belonging to a much later period, is to be seen as I write.

tery-March. This, and every other approach, is commanded by the guns of the fortress.

The royal seat of government is established in the town-house. Sir Edmund and his council meet here.

But something even more detested is established here. Sir Edmund, not being yet able to get into the Puritan churches, — none will consent to it, — has the service of the English Church performed in the town-house. He walks to divine service with a red-coat on one side and the captain of the frigate on the other. Pretty soon, dropping all disguise, he takes forcible possession of the Old South meeting, and has services there, while the Puritan congregation smother their wrath and blow their frozen fingers outside. They cannot go in until his Excellency pleases or has finished his prayers.

Now the first wedding and the first burial ever solemnized or performed with the Episcopal Prayer-Book take place in Boston. At the burial of a man named Lillie, the Episcopal rector, Ratcliffe, attempts but is prevented from reading the burial service by the citizens.

Sir Edmund is evidently a very short-sighted, as well as arbitrary man, or he would use greater discretion in dealing with this people. But if he has any sagacity, he takes care not to show it. To all complaints he has but one answer, "Obey!"

He told the people that they had forfeited their lands with their charter, and must buy them over again. This was to squeeze money out of them for himself and his creatures. He forbade them to assemble in town-meeting, except by his permission. This was to prevent their making formal complaint of their wrongs. He would not allow an appeal to the king to go out of the colony if he could help it; but Rev. Increase Mather, one of the ablest men New England ever saw, did escape in disguise, and so got safely out of his clutches to England.

If in all these things Sir Edmund believed he was doing his duty, the people believed they were doing their own to rid themselves of him and his despotic rule at once and forever. Their ministers told them they were doing God's service at the same time.

The morning of the 18th of April, 1689, dawns in Boston. This day is to have a glorious ending.

Boston has now grown to be a town of seven or eight thousand souls. It contains about three thousand houses, the greater part built of timber covered with shingles; still there are many comely, and for the time, even stately, mansions of brick or stone, having gardens, orchards, and now and then some attempt at ornament, such as a coat-of-arms, carved woodwork, or the like. The people are industrious and frugal. They own ships, which carry the products of the country all over the world. They are now a generation sprung from, and really belonging to, the soil; that is to say, they are now Americans.

FORT HILL, AN INTERLUDE.

At an early hour the people begin to assemble in the streets. Excited and angry faces are everywhere. Boys, armed only with clubs, run about, shouting to each other to fight. Some of the men are armed, some unarmed; but presently, as the loud drums give the expected signal from street to street, all run for their arms, or their rallying points. The quick strokes of church-bells add to the uproar. Up go the colors on the beacon, — the preconcerted signal to the surrounding towns. Then all the country round, from Dorchester to Rumney Marsh, is in a hubbub.

Forming in haste, the military bands march for the town-house. The sword of rebellion is drawn. The persons and papers of those suspected of too much loyalty are seized. Andros, with some of his followers, has taken the alarm in season to escape to the fort. The captain of the frigate is a prisoner in the hands of the insurgents. Joy is in every countenance. By the vociferous huzzas we may measure the weight which has thus been lifted off the neck of a whole people.

But the work of the revolution is only half done. The fort and the frigate together may demolish the town with their broadsides. The ship has run up its colors, opened its ports, and is ready for action. The lieutenant in command swears he will blow the town sky-high. But his captain hastily sends him word that if he fires one shot these same rebels have promised to kill him; and he believes they will perform what they promise. So the frigate's guns are as good as spiked.

Some time is occupied in securing the persons of the most obnoxious members of the late government. A company of soldiers escort the old governor, Simon Bradstreet, to the town-house, where all the principal men, civil and military, are assembled. It is resolved to summon the fort to surrender, and the demand is accordingly made; but Sir Edmund returns a scornful refusal.

Expecting now a desperate and bloody resistance from the fortress, seconded by the frigate, several hours pass by before preparations to attack it are completed. Several thousand men are in arms in King Street, waiting impatiently for the order to march. But the want at this critical moment is not men, it is a leader. At this juncture, when the boldest hesitate, Captain John Nelson, a young gentleman of the town, gallantly puts himself at the head of the soldiers. It is about four in the afternoon when the advance begins.

Dividing in two columns, one body approaches the rear of the fortress, while another moves toward the water-battery. Instead of making any resistance, the royal soldiers, abandoning the battery, run in confusion up the hill to the fort. The sconce, or battery, is immediately occupied by our men, and its guns trained upon the fort itself.

This success happens in the nick of time. It prevents Sir Edmund from escaping on board the frigate, which he was just preparing to do.

All being ready for a final and decisive assault, Captain Nelson now demands, a second time, the surrender of the fort. Its guns are double-shotted with grape, to sweep the hill. To the surprise of all, the demand is acceded to. The gates are thrown open, the insurgents march in, Sir Edmund and his retinue, including "that devil Randolph," as he is called, deliver their swords, the garrison is disarmed, and the revolution successfully ended.

This has been the most tumultuous day Boston has ever witnessed.

The Bostonians have some days of anxiety and excitement, until a ship sails up the harbor bearing the welcome news that William and Mary have been proclaimed King and Queen of England. Then, and not till then, did they breathe freely. They resume, provisionally, their old form of government, the same as before their charter was taken away. Bradstreet, the aged governor, is ninety years old. He is the last of the Puritans, the living link between yesterday and to-day.

In reorganizing the government one man asks nothing and gets nothing.

Captain John Nelson, the man of the hour, is left out in the cold. Why? He is an Episcopalian.

Thus we see that religious tolerance has made no great

progress in fifty-nine years. Already Quakers had been hanged. The Bostonians had only permitted those Episcopalians, who were their fellow-citizens, to hold religious worship, backed by the order of King James, supported by the authority of Andros. They would not sell a foot of land on which an Episcopal church might be built. How singular it seems that religious toleration first came through a tyrannical and arbitrary government, — so arbitrary that the people rose as one man to put it down.

As soon as affairs at home were a little settled, King William granted the colony a new charter. But it is not the old one, as the people had fondly hoped. He is going to appoint the governor, deputy-governor, and secretary, himself, — all the executive officers. The name of "Province" is substituted for that of "Colony." The Assistants are now called Councillors. Some privileges remain in the people; but the charter of King William, the fruit of the revolution, reduces them to a condition of absolute subjection to the throne. The "Governor and Company of the Massachusetts" are no more.

And this is what Fort Hill commemorates, — the dethronement of the House of Stuart, the loss of the ancient charter, and an iron curb on the independent spirit which had steadily grown and flourished under it.

THE BOSTON TRUCK.

V.

LIBERTY-TREE.

IN the year 1646 a man living on the southern skirt of the town planted a young elm-tree.

This was the period of the civil war in England, in which England lost a crown but gained a head. But we do not know that this had anything whatever to do with the tree. In all probability, the man simply planted it for its shade.

Let us say that this tree has been growing one hundred and twenty odd years. Trees were supposed by the ancients to talk: let us go and see what this one has to tell.

We will imagine ourselves in the Boston of Revolutionary times, rebuilding and repeopling it as far as we may. We shall step right into the period most interesting to the great nations of modern times their history has to tell. For all Europe must feel and be disturbed by an uprising of the American colonies. All eyes are therefore turned to Boston, where the revolt is centred. Already the greatest English statesmen are saying, " Oh, if we only had not pushed these Americans too far!"

England tried to find out how much the colonies would bear, and she found it out, to her cost.

England didn't believe the Americans would fight for their rights. But she made a mistake.

England believed that the lion had only to stretch out his gigantic paw and show his great teeth for the Americans to cower like a whipped spaniel at his feet. But the British lion, after gallantly fighting, as he always did, gave up scratching at Yankee forts, which blunted his strong claws, and biting at Yankee bayonets, which broke his sharp teeth, as they had never been blunted and broken before in fair fight.

We should very naturally approach the town over the Neck, still, as in Puritan times, the only avenue over which a road passes.

This neck of land by which the peninsula is attached to the main land was always a bleak and desolate place, over which the wintry winds, and in the season of high tides, the sea also, swept with violence. It had, consequently, caused the early inhabitants great trouble to make and keep in repair a sufficient roadway above high-water mark. In fact, travellers sometimes narrowly escaped drowning while crossing it.

As we have a long and not very interesting way to travel, through the marshes uniting Boston with the mainland, perhaps we had better take a chaise as far as the old fortifications. The landlord of the "George" tavern will furnish the vehicle for a few shillings.

Although

CHAISE OF 1775.

this tavern is one of the noted stopping-places of the province, and boasts the custom of gentlemen of the first rank, we have not the time to try if cellar or larder support this reputation. Our chaise is ready, and our nag impatient to be off.

"My service to you, gentlemen," says the jolly landlord, as we drive from his door.

After leaving the George tavern, standing at the left of the road, near the town's boundary, in the midst of a fine farm, we see nothing except a few travellers, like ourselves, passing in or out, cows grazing contentedly by the roadside, — hear nothing but the occasional pop of a sportsman's gun among the marshes, — until, at the end of half a mile, we come to a group of houses, also at the left hand.[1]

These are the store, house, and barn of Enoch Brown, who has no neighbor on either side nearer than the

EQUESTRIANS, REVOLUTIONARY PERIOD.

tavern we have just left. Here he picks up a little custom from people travelling in or out, particularly from the country folks, who, having sold their garden-stuff, are

[1] In the neighborhood of Blackstone Square.

returning home, jingling the silver in their pockets. At this hour they are going into town with bunches of onions, turnips, or spinach sticking out of the panniers, while Dobbin improves every opportunity to steal a mouthful of fresh grass from the roadside.

Hearing here that the road below is overflowed by the tide, we exchange our chaise for a couple of saddle-horses, and continue our route toward the gates of the town on horseback.

The narrowest part [1] is still the limit of the town, and here the Puritans erected first a gate and then a fortification extending across the Neck so as to securely close the entrance. The gates were constantly guarded, and were shut at a fixed hour in the evening, after which no one was allowed to pass in or out.

MARKET WOMAN, 1775.

Proceeding down the long highway leading from the now dismantled fortification into the town, we find only scattered houses until reaching the corner of Essex Street,

[1] At Dover Street.

where a venerable and spreading elm invites us to halt and partake the cool shade it flings over that antique dwelling behind it.

This is Liberty Tree. This is Liberty Hall.

LIBERTY TREE.

The house is one of the oldest, having been built only thirty-six years after the settlement. But we infer as much from the numerous gables, the overhanging upper story, and the massive chimney-stack, over which the swallows are sharply twittering. Since the year 1727 it has been a printing-office, — first that of John Eliot, and after him, that of his son.

Let us approach this magnificent tree. Ah! there is a large copper plate attached to its trunk. What does it say?

"This tree was planted in the year 1646, and pruned by order of the Sons of Liberty, Feb. 14, 1766."

We will let His Excellency, Governor Bernard, inform us how the tree obtained its name.

"Your lordship must know," he says, in a letter to Lord Hillsborough, "that Liberty Tree is a large old elm in the high street, upon which the effigies were hung in the time of the Stamp Act, and from whence the mobs at that time made their parades. It has since been adorned with an inscription, and has obtained the name of Liberty Tree, as the ground under it has that of Liberty Hall. In August last, just before the commencement of the present troubles, they erected a flag-staff, which went through the tree, and a good deal above the top of the tree. Upon this they hoist a flag as a signal for the Sons of Liberty, as they are called.[1] I gave my Lord Shelburne an account of this erection at the time it was made. This tree has often put me in mind of Jack Cade's Oak of Reformation."

The Stamp Act, we know, was detested, because the colonists were taxed without being allowed any voice in

---

[1] A piece of this flag is now in the Old South collection of Revolutionary relics.

the matter. Parliament assumed that it had this power, — a power claimed to belong naturally and of right to the sovereign. The colonists declared that, while they would willingly tax themselves to raise moneys for the common defence, they could not and would not, sovereign or no sovereign, submit to its being done by a Parliament in which they were allowed no representation. So the cry arose, " No taxation without representation ! " The sovereign people were beginning to assert themselves.

And they did n't submit. They never did submit.

Thus when stamped paper was sent over, and stamp-officers were appointed under the obnoxious Act, the Bostonians made quick work of both. They first mobbed and hung in effigy to this tree the stamp-officer, they then demolished his office, and they finally forced him, on this very spot, publicly, and in presence of a great multitude, to resign his office. The unused stamps, now useless rags, but meant to extort a penny here and sixpence there, for King George to squander, were sent down to the Castle for safe keeping, in order that the exasperated Bostonians might not make a bonfire of them, as they undoubtedly would have done.

Hanging in effigy was a very old way the people had of testifying their displeasure with their rulers. The first use of the kind this tree was put to was on the 14th August, 1765, nearly ten years before active hostilities broke out. At break of day the effigy of Mr. Oliver, the

GENTLEMAN OF THE REVOLUTIONARY DAY.

stamp-officer, and a jack-boot, with the devil, horns and all, peeping out, — a clever hit at Lord Bute, the Prime Minister, — were discovered hanging from Liberty Tree. These images remained hanging all day, and they were visited by great numbers of people, both from the town and the country. All business was suspended. The Lieutenant-Governor (Hutchinson) ordered the sheriff to take the figures down; but the people told him to let them alone, and he obeyed the people.

It was in this way that the tree, which we must agree is a very noble and beautiful symbol of the growth of liberty upon free soil, became the chosen out-of-door resort of the liberty-loving, tyranny-hating Bostonians, until, as times grew worse, necessity obliged them to meet privately.

This spirited action on the part of the Bostonians was quickly followed by the other colonies. In one place a placard was posted up at the street-corner bearing these ominous words: —

"Pro Patria.
"The first man that either distributes or makes use of stamped paper, let him take care of his house, person, and effects."
"We dare.
"Vox Populi."

But the Stamp Act was repealed. The Americans refused to import British goods. This struck right at the pockets of the British merchants. Moreover, they had powerful advocates in Parliament, — men like Barré, Conway, but above all the great Pitt. And let it never be forgotten that the most intrepid spirit during these stormy times Boston knew was James Otis, — a man strong enough and able enough to make himself felt on both sides of the water.[1]

Being in the neighborhood, it would be unpardonable to omit a visit to one of the most eccentric characters of his time, we might also say of any time.

Rev. Mather Byles is the first pastor of Hollis Street Church. A long chapter would be needed to relate all the droll sayings and doings of this witty parson. He lives at the turning of Common Street,[2] not far from his meeting-house, in an old two-story gambrel-roofed dwelling.

OLD HOLLIS STREET.

[1] While Boston was in a state of siege, Liberty Tree was, at the instigation of the Tories, cut down. A soldier, while at work among the branches, fell to the ground, and was killed on the spot. Lafayette said, as he passed it, "The world should never forget the spot where once stood Liberty Tree, so famous in your annals." The stump, long remaining, was used by the people of the neighborhood as a mark of direction. Thus, Samuel Hastings advertises W. I. and New England Rum "at his shop near the stump of Liberty Tree," in 1778. Now a mural tablet perpetuates the site.

[2] The extension of Old, now part of Tremont Street.

But one anecdote we cannot omit, although it carries us far in advance of our time. Still, claiming the historian's privilege, we will narrate it.

The doctor was a Tory, and when the British were driven out of the town he was treated as an enemy. For there are times when no man can stand neutral. He was confined to his own house, and a guard placed over him. On one occasion he persuaded his sentinel to go an errand for him by agreeing to take his place, thus keeping guard *upon himself*. The soldier seemed to appreciate the joke, and handed over his musket to the doctor, who, to the wonder and amusement of all who passed, continued to march gravely up and down before his own door until the soldier's return. The authorities afterwards relieved the guard from this duty; then they put it back; and then finally freed the witty doctor from it altogether. But have his joke he would at their expense. He declared that he had been *guarded*, regarded, and disregarded.

VI.

A TEMPEST IN A BIG TEA-POT.

CHANCE has led us to the spot on which the house of Governor Winthrop stands. But by the side of it, in a crowded neighborhood, is a brick church, with a fine and lofty steeple pricking the frosty air of a December afternoon. There is a dense crowd of men, with a sprinkling of women, arguing and gesticulating about the door, but the interior is so choked up with people that we can scarcely elbow our way in. The men's faces, we notice, are flushed and excited, and there is an angry buzz of half-suppressed voices. Evidently something out of the common has brought these people here. What can it be?

Ah! they are all talking about tea.

"You can lead a horse to water, but you can't make him drink," one says, very significantly, to his neighbor.

"Aye, and they can send us tea, but can't make us drink," responded his neighbor.

"Let them take it back to England, then, and peddle it out there," ejaculates a third. "We will not have it forced down our throats," he adds.

OLD SOUTH.

"What sort of a drink would tea and salt water make?" suggests a man who is evidently losing patience; for it has grown dark, and the lamps shed a dim light throughout the unquiet crowd.

"Good for John Rowe!" shout the bystanders approvingly, and, as his words pass from mouth to mouth, the people laugh and clap.

Presently a man of middle age speaks. At his first words every voice is hushed. Every eye is turned upon him. In a grave and steady voice he tells the people that

A TEMPEST IN A BIG TEA-POT.

their purpose to send the tea-ships home to England, with their cargoes untouched, has been thwarted by Governor Hutchinson, who refuses to give the vessels the pass, without which they cannot sail. "And now," concludes this same grave and earnest voice, to which all eagerly listen, "this meeting can do nothing more to save the country."

There is a moment's silence, — a moment of keen disappointment, an ominous silence.

Then some one in the gallery cries out, in a ringing voice, "Boston Harbor a tea-pot to-night! Hurrah for Griffin's Wharf!"

Instantly, before the people are aware what is intended, an Indian war-whoop pierces the air; and, starting at the signal, no one seems to know whence or how, half a hundred men, having their faces smeared with soot, and disguised as Indian warriors, brandishing hatchets and shouting as they run, pour through Milk Street, followed by the crowd, turn down to Griffin's Wharf, where the tea-ships lay, clamber on board, take off the hatches in a  hurry, and while some pass up the chests from the hold others smash and pitch them overboard. Crash go the hatchets, splash goes the tea. Splash! splash! Every one works for dear life, earnest and determined.

Never were ships more quickly unloaded. The frightened captains and crews were told to go below and stay there if they would not be harmed. They obeyed. No one but the fishes drank that tea.

After finishing their work the lads who have been making a tea-pot of Boston Harbor marched gayly back to town to the music of a fife. While on their way they passed by the residence of Mad Montagu, the British admiral, who commanded all the fleet of war-ships then lying at anchor within gunshot of the town. The admiral threw up his window, thrust out his head, and hallooed: —

"Well, boys, you have had a fine, pleasant evening for your Indian caper, have n't you? But mind, you 've got to pay the fiddler yet!"

"Oh, never mind, Squire!" shouted Pitts, the leader. "Just come out here, if you please, and we'll settle the bill in two minutes."

The admiral shut his window in a hurry, and the tea-party, with a laugh for the admiral, marched on. He was fond of a fight, but thought it best to decline this invitation.

But who, we ask, was the man whose words carried with them so much authority at the meeting, and whom everybody seemed instinctively to look upon as their leader?

That man, we are told, was Samuel Adams.

And who was Samuel Adams?

Why, Samuel Adams was the Man of THE REVOLUTION.

He was one of themselves. That is why the people trusted him. He believed in them. That is why they believed in him. He had great ability to plan, firmness to execute, and was devoted heart and soul to the cause of his country. He had a will of iron. He was poor, but unselfish. He did not ask any reward. He believed first in God and next in his country. He was one of the old Puritans whom nothing could turn from a purpose once fixed,— no, not even bribes, nor threats, nor danger to life and limb. Washington was the head of the army. Samuel Adams was the head of the people.

Why, only a few years before, two British regiments had been sent out to overawe this people. Their presence in the town very soon led to bloodshed. The soldiers, infuriated by taunts, fired upon the citizens, killing several on the spot. Thus did the prophetic words of Franklin, when he was asked in the House of Lords about sending the military to enforce the Stamp Act — "The troops will not find a rebellion: they may, indeed, make one" — come true. They did make one. Franklin knew.

The enraged Bostonians, after this deplorable affair happened, would have torn the two regiments in pieces. They demanded the removal of the troops from the town. Thomas Hutchinson, the acting governor, tried to defeat this purpose by equivocation, but Adams sternly forced him to obey the will of an outraged people. The troops were sent out of town. And the British minister, Lord

North, after he heard of it, always spoke contemptuously of these soldiers as Sam Adams's two regiments.

The people's friend and champion is never himself friendless. Adams was poor; yes, and proud too. Not being rich, he could not and did not associate with the wealthy Hancocks, Bowdoins, Higginsons, and Russells. His dress and his manners were equally modest and plain. But the people loved him, and this was their way of showing it. He had neglected money-getting to help them in their struggle against tyranny, and Bostonians are never ungrateful.

His old barn being ready to fall, some persons, who would not tell their names, asked permission to build him a new one. He consented, and it was done in a few days. Another asked leave to repair his house. This was also thoroughly done. Another friend sent to beg him, as a favor, to call at a tailor's shop and be measured for a suit of clothes. Still another gave him a new wig; and others a new hat, hose, and shoes enough to last him the rest of his life. Then some one else finished up this donation with a purse containing fifteen or twenty broad pieces of gold.

All this was done with as much delicacy of feeling as if the givers had belonged to the highest rank of society. Samuel Adams did not demean himself by accepting these gifts any more than a soldier does by receiving his pay, or a general his pension.

This was Adams's way of telling the people how they

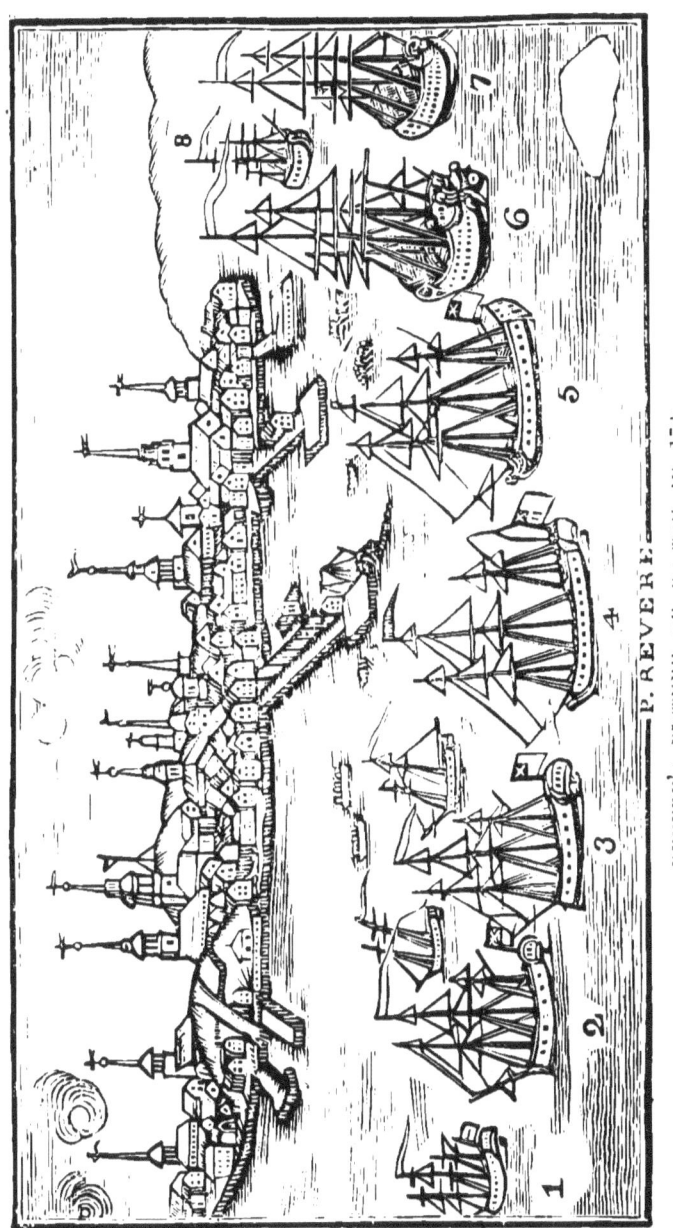

P. REVERE'S PICTURE OF BOSTON IN 1768.

might dare even the power of the mighty British Empire. He told them a fable like this one: —

"A Greek philosopher, who was lying asleep on the grass, was suddenly aroused by a sharp pain in the palm of his hand. He shut his hand quickly and found he had caught a little field-mouse. While he was looking at it, and wondering how such an insignificant animal dared to attack him, it bit him a second time. He dropped it and it made its escape. Now, fellow citizens," said Adams, "there is no animal, however weak and contemptible, which cannot defend its own liberty if it will only *fight* for it."

THE HEART AND CROWN.

Now I think we know who Samuel Adams was.

As we walk about, we are not a little amused by the odd signs hanging on iron cranes over the shop or tavern doors. Many of them display great ingenuity to attract custom. Here, for instance, is a printer's and bookseller's sign, The Heart and Crown.[1] Here is one hung out by a dealer in English and India goods, The Three Doves.[2]

A third, with the date, is The Blue Ball, the sign of

---

[1] The sign of T. Fleet, in old Cornhill, or at the north corner of Water and Washington Streets.

[2] The sign of Wm. Blair Townsend, in Marlborough, now Washington Street.

Benjamin Franklin's father.[1] A still more curious one is that of a tavern on the Neck, on which, as shown in the picture, is a man, with head, one arm, and leg sticking out through a globe, like a chicken breaking its shell. From the man's mouth issue the words "How shall I get through this world?"[2]

Some other signs are the Golden Cock, Crown and Sceptre, Dish of Lemons, Bunch of Grapes, Cross Keys, Black Boy and Butt, Dog and Rainbow, Cromwell's Head, etc.[3]

THREE DOVES.

The neighborhood of the Old South is rich in historical associations. On one side, as we have said, is the home of Governor Winthrop; on the other, in Milk Street, facing the church, is the birthplace of that eminent citizen, statesman, and philosopher, Benjamin Franklin. The house has been shown in a preced-

---

[1] At the corner of Hanover and Union Streets; the building was demolished in 1858 to widen the street.

[2] An anecdote is told of this sign. It is said that during the Revolutionary War a Continental regiment halted in front of this tavern after a forced march from Providence. The men were ready to drop from fatigue, but could not help laughing at the droll figure on the signboard; and one of the soldiers reading the inscription, "How shall I get through this world?" exclaimed, "'List! darn ye, 'list! and you'll get through soon enough." This sally put the men in a good humor, for soldiers dearly love a joke at all times.

[3] The Bunch of Grapes is still hanging in South Market Street.

ing chapter, but here is a representation of the very press on which he worked as a journeyman printer.[1] For centuries the printing-press has scarcely been altered, and this one is, as nearly as may be, an exact model of that used by William Caxton, in 1471, in England.[2]

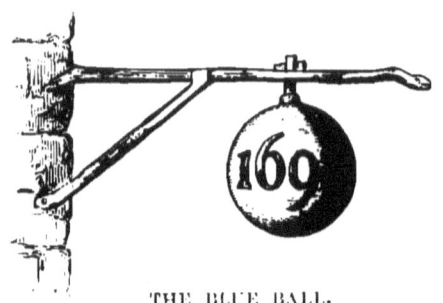

THE BLUE BALL.

Turning now to the opposite side of Old Marlborough Street we see, standing some distance back from it, a fine, stately building, built of brick. We see on the portico of the entrance the arms of Great Britain. Glancing upward, the bronze figure of an Indian, in the act of fitting an arrow to his bow, glistens brightly on the pinnacle of the cupola. The arms denote an official residence. This is the mansion house of the royal governors, or Province House.[3]

"HOW SHALL I GET THROUGH THIS WORLD?"

---

[1] On exhibition in the collection of the Old South.

[2] Learn something about Caxton and the art of printing. See Thomas's History of Printing for the rise of this art in America.

[3] Arms and Indian are now in possession of the Mass. Hist. Society. For particular directions concerning the sites of these old buildings, consult Old Landmarks of Boston, and Middlesex.

A TEMPEST IN A BIG TEA-POT. 83

At the time of the outbreak we have lately witnessed in the Old South, the acting Governor, having a house of his own at the North End, did not live here. But we will call on him by and by.

With its handsome grass lawn in front, shaded by stately trees, and separated by a fence from the highway; with its paved walk leading from the gateway up to the broad stone steps, over which we should tread with a becoming sense of the dignity we are approaching; with its sentinel in scarlet pacing up and down the corridor like an automaton; with the orderlies lounging here, booted and spurred; with the horses ready saddled at the porter's lodge,— we should, in a few short months after the memorable Tea Party, see the peaceful abode of the earlier governors, who lived here in quiet state, changed into a military headquarters, with General Thomas Gage in possession. For now the town has been declared in open rebellion, and all its shipping prohibited from setting sail, by the passage of the Boston

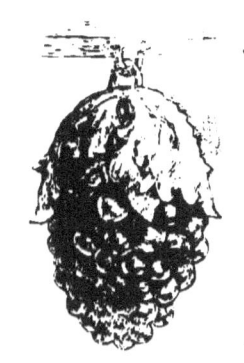

BUNCH OF GRAPES.

FRANKLIN'S PRESS.

Port Bill in Parliament, assembled. George III. is furious.

And all for pitching that unlucky tea overboard.

I pray you, my young reader, to pay no attention to those writers who continue, even yet, to call the British

THE PROVINCE HOUSE.

outcasts, felons, or murderers. The officers were as brave, as chivalric even, the soldiers as good, as those of any army. They and our fathers were now enemies, but they had been friends and comrades. They began war by making a terrible mistake. Because some imbecile had said the Yankees were all cowards, most of the young soldiers believed it. But the graybeards, like General Gage, knew better. They had fought side by side with those despised Yankees, at Havana, Louisburg, Quebec, and "Ty." These men shook their heads sadly when they heard the youngsters of the army say, with a supercilious sniff: —

"'Pon my life, I believe there does not exist so great a set of rascals and poltroons as these same Yankees!"

The poor fellow who made that silly speech lived to repent it. A Yankee bullet pierced his breast in less than a year.

But the Bostonians hated the soldiers just as cordially, and it did them good to call them opprobrious names when speaking of them. It did them good to cudgel them soundly when they caught them without their arms.

General Gage was not a bad man. Far from it. But King George told him to crush out rebellion in Massachusetts, as if it was the easiest thing in the world. He had served a long time in America, and carried a French bullet he had received at Braddock's defeat. He had only just returned to England from Boston when the king sent for him.

"About these rebellious Bostonians?" said George III.

"Oh, your Majesty," the general replied, "they will be lions while we are lambs; but if we take the resolute part they will undoubtedly prove very meek."

"And how many of my soldiers will be necessary to bring them to their senses?"

"Four regiments, sire, will be more than sufficient."

"Very good, sir. I mean to send you there."

"I shall be ready at a day's notice, your Majesty," answered General Gage, bowing low.

So he took his American wife under his arm and came to Boston, with a smiling face, but, I'll be bound, a heavy heart beating under his gold-embroidered coat. The people liked General Gage: they considered him half American at least, for he had fought with Washington and Putnam, and had married, as we know, a high-spirited American lady. But they were now bent on war. So this general tried to be a generous enemy. He was as slow to begin the "crushing" as possible, — so slow that his soldiers grew angry with him. His officers teased him to begin. His king said, with a sneer, that he was "too amiable." And presently General Gage found himself disgraced, and ordered to give up the command to General William Howe, the fire-eater and lady-killer.

Perhaps you have heard that even in these old times the Boston boys were in the habit of coasting on the Common. They would build hills of snow and slide swiftly down to the Frog Pond. Well, the English soldiers had their camps on the Common, and from mere love of mischief would, when the boys had gone to school, destroy their coasting-ground. Incensed at having their sport thus meanly prevented, a delegation of boys went to General Gage about it. When shown into his presence he asked, with surprise, why so many children had come to see him.

"We come, sir," said the young spokesman, with a flushed face, "to ask a redress of our grievances."

"What!" said the general, "have your fathers been teaching you rebellion, and sent you here to utter it?"

"Nobody sent us, sir," replied the brave little fellow. "We have never injured or insulted your soldiers, but they have trodden down our snow-hills, and broken the ice on our skating-ground. We complained, and they called us young rebels, and told us to help ourselves if we could. Yesterday our works were destroyed for the third time, and now," said the lad, with flashing eyes, "we will bear it no longer."

General Gage looked at the boys with undisguised admiration. Then, turning to an officer who stood near, he exclaimed: —

"Good heavens! the very children draw in a love of liberty with the air they breathe." To the lads he then said: —

"You may go, my brave boys; and be assured that if any of my troops hereafter molest you, they shall be severely punished."

THE OLD CORNER.

VII.

FROM THE OLD CORNER TO KING STREET.

LET us now turn back a little as far as School Street, so as to continue our walk by Tremont Street and Prison Lane to King Street.

The northerly corner of School Street is occupied by a brick house, plain and portly. It is only a store, with a dwelling overhead, as the custom is. But ere we pass it by with only a glance, we remember that on the spot where it stands was the home of the unfortunate Anne Hutchinson, who was banished for what were termed her heresies. She was, however, a very sensible woman, whose crime consisted in thinking out for herself the way of salvation. So she had to go the way of Roger Williams, — an outcast and a wanderer, flying from Christians to savages for freedom of conscience.

She brought around her, in her house, the most notable Bostonians of her day, such as Vane, Cotton, and Wheelwright, and was fast making converts to her own opinions when the Puritan ministers bitterly denounced her. Deserted by her friends, her conduct was heroic. She, at least, would not renounce her opinions, her convictions rather, but remained firm. So greatly were the authorities alarmed that all those inhabitants who were supposed to sympathize with her were disarmed. This was the greatest religious commotion that ever occurred in Boston.[1]

Passing the Latin School, from which the street takes its name, we continue to ascend, coming shortly to a massive and gloomy building of stone standing at the corner of Tremont, or Treamount Street as it is still called, in the Revolutionary days. A square bell-tower, rising above the roof, gives entrance to the building. It looks a perpetual defiance to Puritanism, — a fortress of the old faith. This is King's Chapel, in which Captain-General Gage and his suite come to church. Going in, we find the pew,

[1] The causes are too intricate for young readers to understand. Indeed, one hardly knows whether to be most incredulous or ashamed of such relentless persecution.

conspicuous for its size and elegance, set apart for the
royal governor, in which he sits and listens to the reading
of the Litany by the rector, Dr. Caner. The pride of
birth, and station, and loyalty to the throne well suited
the traditions of this Church. Prayers are read from a

KING'S CHAPEL.

book having the royal monogram, "G. R.," thereon. An
organ, selected it is said by the great Handel himself,
blazoned with golden crown and mitre, peals forth the
Te Deum. The walls are hung around with the proud
armorial badges of those old families who have founded
an aristocracy in Puritan Boston, and who ride to church

in chariots with liveried black footmen standing up behind. Powdered wigs, costly laces, satin or velvet robes, with here and there a scarlet coat, glow like a bed of flowers against the cold gray walls. Proud patrician faces look up, and red lips utter, with emphasis, the responses while the prayer to save our sovereign lord the King is being read. These loyalists are called by the patriots, as a reproach, Tories.

A HACKNEY COACH.

But for all that there were patriots in this church, too, who, we doubt not, offered up a silent prayer for their distressed country. These were called Whigs.

SHIRLEY ARMS.

Here, outside the massive walls, mounded with graves and thick with their last monuments, is the ancient graveyard of the Puritans. While we have been inspecting the emblems of the living, those of the dead now meet the eye. Some are of lead and imbedded in freestone slabs; some cut with much skill in hard slate-stone.[1] Were we to descend into the tombs we should find these arms engraved on the silver coffin-plates. But enough of these frail relics of a frail humanity.

At the other extremity of the burial-ground we find the old wooden house in which Dr. Caner, rector of King's Chapel, lives. We now turn the corner of Queen Street.[2] Keeping the right hand, we come first to the parsonage of Brattle Street Church, then to the Court House and Prison.

The Court House is a new brick building with an octagonal cupola. The Prison is a large stone building, of three stories, having brick partitions, strongly cased with plank and iron. It is not nearly so squalid or so forbidding as the old prison of Puritan times, in which so many miserable ones languished. That had thick stone walls, dark corridors, and cold, damp dungeons. But the old forms of punishment are still employed, except that death is not now inflicted for certain offences under the old Judaic law. Thieves and housebreakers are branded in the hand, or on both cheeks, with a hot iron, and so compelled to wear the badge of infamy through life. Sitting on the gallows, or in the

---

[1] Look along the railing, next the sidewalk, for some of these ancient escutcheons.

[2] Now Court. First called Prison Lane. The corner house was once occupied by General Washington.

stocks, or so many stripes on the bare back, are usual in common offences.

Emerging from Queen Street we have directly in front the old Court House, in which the General Court or Legislature sits, or did sit until General Gage summoned it to meet at Salem, when, having first locked the door against Mr. Secretary Flucker who came to dissolve it, the members formed themselves into a Provincial Congress. "We have the name of rebels, and might as well have the game, too," they think.

The secretary, finding the door shut in his face, sheepishly read the proclamation on the stairs to a few gaping idlers.

Once more we stand in the heart of old Boston. We find it much changed. The wooden Town-House, first erected here, has given place to this more imposing structure. The first Puritan meeting-house has been removed from its ancient location, and now fronts Cornhill, a little way to our right. Far down King Street we see tapering masts and sparkling water. On the corner opposite

OLD STATE HOUSE.

to us is the shop of Henry Knox,[1] stationer and bookbinder.

Going now as far as the open space at the lower end of the Court, or Town-House, we stand on the spot made memorable by the Fifth of March Massacre. At our left, as we look down the street, hangs the sign of the Royal Exchange Tavern, one of the best in the town. Looking up, the arms of the kingdom — the lion and the unicorn, the red-cross shield — grace each angle of the town-house tower. We are in the centre of trade, at the junction of the two principal thoroughfares of the town. The lower floor of the Town-House has been used by the merchants, ever since the old days, as their exchange. But where now is the old activity, the throng, the bustle, of a year ago? Few people and fewer vehicles are in the streets. The men look downcast

SPEAKER'S DESK.

OLD BRICK CHURCH.

---

[1] Afterwards the Revolutionary general.

and preoccupied, the women look brave but sad; the warehouses are deserted, the merchants sit idle in their stores. This is the effect of the Port Bill. Grass grows in the streets. The king means to starve the Bostonians into submission. Will he do it?

TROPHIES OF BENNINGTON.

VIII.

THE ROYAL BEAST SHOWS HIS TEETH.

THE venerable building, in whose shadow we are, is a speaking monument of the days "that tried men's souls." Its walls have rung with the fiery eloquence of an Otis, and they have shaken with the murderous volleys poured into the breasts of the Sons of Liberty. "Here," says John Adams, "Independence was born." With what pride should Bostonians, pointing to this building in the future, repeat to the stranger, "Here Independence was born"! With what shame would they hang their heads if they could only point to the vacant spot of ground in silence![1]

[1] This old building has been the scene of events more vital to the history of Boston and New England — I may say of the whole

But while we have been musing here, our ears are saluted by the crash of martial music. We look down the street to see it choked up with glittering bayonets over which the free breeze unfurls the proud standards that have floated victorious over many a hard-fought field of the Old World.

Hark to the roll of the drums! Listen to the bugles! They come nearer. Now we see the bearskins of the grenadiers. They know that a thousand eyes are upon them. Their bearing shows it. The king's crest and cipher glitter on the front of their caps. The king's cipher within the garter, with the crown above, is in the centre of their colors, and upon their drums. They wear his livery. Other regiments are the king's, but this one is the "King's Own."

The negro drummer-boys look like dressed-up monkeys. So the crowd thinks, and laughs. But hark! what is the band playing? Can it be? Yes, it is "Yankee Doodle," played in derision. Now the lookers-on do not laugh. They are ominously silent.

How bravely the young officers look, in their ruffles and gold lace! Many are younger sons of nobles and peers who hardly have a serious thought for anything. Swords bright,

country — than any other now standing in the city of the Puritans. If there is any pile of brick and stone within its limits worth preserving, it is this one; and if there is any spot to which a reverence of the great past calls us, it is here.

hearts light, they march airily along. They glance scornfully around, for they have been told these bloodthirsty Bostonians would not let them step foot on the sacred soil. Perhaps they see a pretty face at a window, and gallantly touch their laced beavers. Perhaps their eyes meet a scowling one, and return a haughty stare of defiance. These thousand Englishmen, whose steady tramp shakes the solid earth, believe themselves invincible. They are the sons of the heroes of Crecy, and Agincourt, and Quebec! They will march through or over thousands of such rabble as they see sternly watching their fine parade, they think. They have come three thousand miles to do it. Rebellion is to be put down. The king shall have his own. Old England to the rescue!

"What regiment is that? By St. George, it is a right royal one, indeed!"

"That is the King's Own Regiment."

"Well," drawls a bystander, who has been watching them intently, "they are trim-looking lads, to be sure; but an ounce of lead would settle one of them just as quick as another man, I'm thinking."

"And did you notice the lion on their ensign, how fat and sleek he looks?" asked another.

"Aye, a pampered beast,— needs blood-letting," replied the bold citizen who has just spoken.

"Curse them! I wish the earth would open and swallow every mother's son," mutters a rabid rebel.

THE ROYAL BEAST SHOWS HIS TEETH.

The battalion moves on through Queen and Tremont Streets to the Common. Here it halts. The companies wheel into line, colors are planted, muskets stacked, sentinels posted. They are then dismissed. Men from each company begin to mark off their campground, and to set up their tents. A poor, frightened cow — the men stone her and shout — runs blindly into the line of stacked arms and wounds herself upon the bayonets.

REGIMENTAL ENSIGN TAKEN AT YORKTOWN.

One by one a cloud of tents arise on the green. A village in white seems sprung from the greensward. The women and camp-followers bring fagots and light fires, over which pots are soon cooking supper for this thousand-mouthed hydra. Colonel Madison turns his bridle-rein and rides to the Province House to make his report, and mayhap to taste General Gage's Madeira.

While this is going on the officers gather in little groups to talk over the events of the day. They say: —

"So here we are at last." "We've marched through Boston and not burnt a kernel of powder, in spite of all their threats." "But what a lovely spot." "This west

100　　　　　AROUND THE HUB.

SENTRY GO.

breeze across the bay!" "Those trees for a morning promenade!" "This smooth turf for parade."

Thus they keep up a running fire of comments until their servants, of which each has one or more, call them to the mess-tables.

"Very pretty, very pretty indeed," growls a beardless sub over his rasher. "This will do well enough for a lark, but there's a deuced better chance to sell out and turn farmer than for promotion, I'm thinking."

"Wait a bit, my boy," returns a veteran officer, "wait a bit. It's easy enough to get into a trap, but either I'm an idiot or we shall get singed before we get out."

Then they all laugh and grow merry at the last speaker's expense. But they don't know that the men who sullenly watched their parade have gone home to run bullets, and to whet their fathers' swords.

This is the fourteenth day of June, 1774. The Bostonians have sowed sedition and are reaping a crop of steel.

On the next day the 43d lands; then the 5th and 38th, with six pieces of cannon. Earl Percy, colonel of the 5th, scion of a noble house, takes command of this camp, and General Gage — for he was beginning to feel downright uneasy — and the Tories too, breathe more freely. The Bostonians breathe between their teeth.

So far the British have done nothing but drive the cows from their old pastures; and no blood has been spilt, except that of the poor animal who ran off with a bayonet sticking in her ribs, bellowing with fright.

Having followed the soldiers to the Common, — we all love to follow the soldiers dearly, — nothing prevents our looking about us.

We are standing in the Mall, which is the only portion of the Common used as a promenade by the citizens, or planted with shade-trees. But this extends only a little below Winter Street. All the rest is uncared for, and perhaps treeless, except that one gigantic elm near the Frog Pond, which, could it speak, as the ancients pretended the trees could, might tell us of many things it has witnessed.[1] For here it was growing when the first Eng-

---

[1] This "Great Elm," long so-called, was blown down during a severe gale, the night of Feb. 15, 1876.

lish came to found their city in the wilderness. Behind it rises a little hill. By its side is the miry pool called

THE GREAT ELM.

the Frog Pond. West of us the green slopes ascend gently to the summit of Beacon Hill, on which stands the signal mast, or beacon, as in the olden time.

A little way down the slope, towards us, is a fine colonial mansion. Recollect this house, for it is the residence of John Hancock, Esq., a Boston rebel. We have now taken a general view of the Common.

But the Mall, though short, we see is extended northerly

THE GREAT MALL, HAYMARKET, AND THEATRE IN 1795.

towards King's Chapel by a row of beautiful elm-trees[1] planted by Adino Paddock, and from him called Paddock's Mall. And he also gave the name of Long Acre to that part of Tremont Street from School to Winter. Adino Paddock is a coach and chariot builder.

> "A train-band captain eke was he
> Of famous Boston town."

He commands the town's artillery-train. He is a red-hot Tory.

Paddock's Mall skirts the Old Granary Burying-ground, so-called because the town Granary, a long, wooden building stands at the corner beside it, where the street[2] ascends Beacon Hill. The town Almshouse and Workhouse are on this street, adjoining the Granary.

We finish our investigation just in the nick of time, for a group of military gentlemen is approaching. It is General Gage and his retinue. First marches His Excellency, stout, pompous, and wearing an enormous cocked-hat, looped up at the side with golden buttons. In his hand is a light cane over which the sleeve-ruffles negligently droop. His face is clean shaven, for the regulation of the army forbids wearing a beard. A big shirt-frill, stiff with starch, sticks out of his bosom like a fin. A

---

[1] Notwithstanding urgent remonstrance from all classes of citizens the city authorities, a few years ago, caused these trees to be cut down. No sufficient reason was given for the act.

[2] Park Street, formerly "Centry" or Sentry Street.

scarlet coat with gold epaulets, a long, buff waistcoat, breeches fitting the leg tightly, white silk stockings, feet encased in high shoes adorned with silver buckles, make up the outward man of the British commander-in-chief. Take a good look at him. He has promised to put down rebellion with four battalions.

The general is attended by five or six field-officers, two or three aide-de-camps, with eight orderly sergeants following at a very respectful distance. They must not overhear anything. Evidently he is going to pay a visit of ceremony.

An antique wooden house, rising in the midst of a delightful garden, that extends far down Winter Street on one side, and back towards the Granary on the other, occupies the corner opposite to us. Into this house the general goes, while officers of high and low degree kick their heels at the gate, forming two little groups, indicating the difference between the general and the colonel, the colonel and the sergeant. This is military etiquette: keep your distance.

The house belongs to Inspector Williams,[1] a crown officer, perhaps. It is at present the headquarters of my Lord Percy, who, though the possessor of a great name, will do very little, we think, towards making it greater. It is

---

[1] It was afterwards the residence of Samuel Breck, agent of the French Government, and a successful Boston merchant. It had also been occupied by Governor Sir Francis Bernard.

only a step from this house to the camp. The general is going to visit the earl. His earlship, it is true, obeys General Gage's orders here, but at home he is the greater man of the two. He will inherit vast wealth. Consequently, General Gage does not call him "colonel," but "my lord," and says, "How is your lordship to-day?" and he "my lords" him until we are a good deal puzzled to know which is the general and which the colonel. But this also is etiquette, of another kind. They call it caste. General Gage knows full well that the Percy has more influence in England than he, a hundred times over. So the poor general has bigger men than himself under him, and he feels it.

But this proud earl, with his long nose, his weak eyes, and his long legs, treats his 5th Regiment munificently. Therefore, to a man, the regiment adores him. Of course he is brave: he is a Percy. But his superiors must handle his earlship very gingerly indeed. A live lord is something very sacred to Englishmen.

We have the troops and their commanders settled at last; and now we will cross over the Common, keeping outside the line of sentinels, to the elegant mansion house spoken of as the residence of John Hancock, Esq. This John Hancock is a wealthy merchant. He inherited wealth; he also inherited this house, built by his rich uncle, Thomas, from his aunt Lydia. He rides in his chariot, gives elegant suppers, and lives generally like a prince. His house is crammed with costly furniture and beautiful paintings. He is well educated, and has travelled abroad. John Hancock, though a minister's son, and a rich man through trade, is a part of the upper crust. But underneath the crust is the meat. He can open his window of a morning, and letting in the sun, look down over the white tents of the army sent to subjugate his country and his people.

HANCOCK MANSION.

He can look over these to the wooden house occupied by the deputy-commandant, — the titled soldier of Britain. But he did not see a prouder man than himself there, if all we hear is true.

But which side will he choose?

Hancock became an ardent patriot, an honest one too. But he had to be managed, coaxed, and flattered. He was not another Samuel Adams, a patriot by the inspiration of freedom alone. Not he. But then, there could hardly be two Samuel Adamses in the same century. Really, there could be very little sympathy between these two men till the king, by declaring them the two greatest traitors in all his broad realm, bound them together forever; and there they will stand in history, — Hancock and Adams, the proscribed rebels.

But now John Hancock is an especial object of hatred to the British army. According to one royal officer, he is "a poor, contemptible fool led about by Adams."

Having talked of the owner, let us look at the house, — the best, everything considered, in Boston.

The building is of stone, built in the substantial manner favored by the wealthier Bostonians, with very thick walls. A balcony projects over the entrance door upon which a large window of the second story opens. The corners and windows are ornamented with Braintree granite. The roof is tiled and surmounted by a balustrade. Dormer windows, jutting out from this roof, give a beautiful and extensive view of town and harbor. A low stone wall, with a light wooden fence placed upon it, separates the grounds from the street. A paved walk, then a dozen stone steps, conduct to the mansion, situated on rising ground a little back from the street. Before the door is a broad stone slab worn by the feet of the distinguished inhabitant and his guests. [1]

As the different regiments arrive they take position on the right of the 4th, or "King's Own," whose camp is directly opposite the quarters of Earl Percy. Thus we have Boston under bayonet rule.

[1] For a further description see Old Landmarks of Boston, pp. 338-343.

The citizens have never given themselves the trouble to hide their detestation of the soldiery. They recollect the 5th of March. The soldiers treat the citizens with contempt or violence whenever they meet in the streets. Both are "spoiling" for a fight. But for a while they will limit themselves to knock-downs and fisticuffs.

Soldiers and citizens, King's Men and Liberty Boys, begin to abuse each other directly. From words they quickly get to blows. Sometimes one, sometimes the other, gets the worst. The soldiers generally begin the street affrays, but as by and by the parties grow more and more exasperated, General Gage wisely forbids his soldiers wearing their side-arms about the town. Then they catch it. Then they begin to call their general such names as "Tommy" and "The Old Woman," because he will not let them cut and stab and beat these rascal Bostonians as much as they like.

Officers who get tipsy over their cards and their bottle will also jostle the townspeople and insult their wives. Then a lively "scrimmage" takes place, in which more than once the officers, after drawing their hangers, not only have them taken away by force, but have their epaulets torn off and trampled under foot. To his honor, General Gage is very indignant when his officers behave so unbecomingly. He does all he can; but there is "an irrepressible conflict" going on, and he is carried along in the current as helplessly as a baby.

If we may believe report it is not long since an odd adventure happened to some of his Majesty's officers who were out taking a stroll on Beacon Hill after sunset. The first they knew something whizzed close to their heads. Then the air was filled with buzzing noises which they took to be bullets flying from unseen guns. They could not imagine these noises were made by the big dor-beetle, which is so stupid and so helpless, but, taking to their heels, these valiant sons of Mars fled down the hill into the camp, where they spread the report that they had been shot at by Yankee air-guns. And this ridiculous story was actually written home to England as sober truth. Some pretend that the Americans possess a magic powder, which explodes without making any report at all.

That celebrated wit, McFingal, did not lose such a chance as this to satirize the officers in verse: —

> "No more the British colonel runs
> From whizzing beetles as air-guns;
> Thinks horn-bugs bullets, or thro' fear
> Musketoes takes for musketeers:
> Nor 'scapes as if you'd gained supplies
> From Beelzebub's whole host of flies,
> No bug these warlike hearts appals;
> They better knew the sound of balls."

IX.

A GARRISONED TOWN.

MORE troops. More bayonets. The 59th disembarks. General Gage sends it at once to fortify Boston Neck. The whole colony is now intensely excited by the presence of the British army, for army it is. It is arming. It is getting its blood up. Nothing will bring so high a price as a musket, a sword, or a cannon. Everywhere regiments of minute-men are forming and drilling. The village parsons are in the ranks with the rest. Plainly, it is going to be bayonet against bayonet, brother against brother. So General Gage is fortifying. He scents war.

The Royal Welsh Fusileers arrive, and go into camp on Fort Hill. Now troops are coming thick and fast, — from New York, from Quebec, from Newfoundland, from Ireland. The 64th takes possession of and garrisons the Castle. The Royal Marine Battalion is quartered in the North End. A guard is placed at the Charlestown Ferry, a frigate anchored in the channel, and every night the ferry-boats are taken alongside so that deserters cannot get out, or rebels get in. The 47th, the 52d, the 10th, and part of the 18th again strongly reinforce the army. Nothing now but bugles and drums and the tramp of armed men from morn till night. General Gage has seized the powder and cannon belonging to the province. He is disarming the Bostonians. But Yankee wit and Yankee courage rise with the emergency. The Bostonians seize and spirit away under the very noses of his grand army the cannon belonging to their artillery company. Two can play at that game. This is the way it was done.

The gun-house, where the cannon were kept, stood opposite the Mall, at the corner of West Street, and of course opposite the camp of the King's Own. There was then a noble elm-tree on this spot. The next building was a schoolhouse. Both buildings were enclosed by the same fence, — a high one.

Paddock, the Tory major, had been overheard to say he would deliver his guns to General Gage. As a precaution General Gage posted sentinels around the gun-house until he should be ready to remove the two field-pieces. But the thought that they were in danger never, perhaps, entered his mind.

One morning when the British artillerymen came to take them away, what was their astonishment to find them missing. There, to be sure, were the carriages; but where the guns?

"They're gone! I'll be hanged if these rebels won't

A GARRISONED TOWN. 113

steal the teeth out of your head, and you keeping guard!" roared the sergeant.

Yet the sentinels swore they had neither seen nor heard anything, although one of them was placed at the gun-house door.

The bold fellows, who had resolved that General Gage should not have the guns, but the Americans should have them by hook or by crook, got into the yard through the schoolhouse. Once in the yard they lifted the latch of the gun-house door through a crevice, and stole in on tiptoe. Still and watchful, they waited until the sentry at the outer door had his attention taken off by the roll-call in the camp. Then silently lifting the guns off their carriages the workmen quickly carried them into the schoolhouse, putting them into a large box in which fire-wood was kept. This box was under the master's desk. They then stole away, leaving everything as they found it.

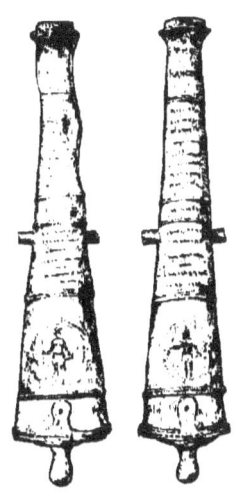

THE GUNS "HANCOCK AND ADAMS."

Well, the guns were missed. Search was instantly made. The soldiers went into the school-room, but out of consideration for the master, who had a lame foot, which he carefully kept on the wood-box, they did not disturb that. Several school-boys were present who knew just

8

where the guns were hid, but they did not lisp one word, nor did they, during the fortnight the guns remained there, betray the secret. So much for the Boston boys.

At the end of this time the guns were carried to a blacksmith's shop at the South End and buried under a coal-heap. Afterwards they were safely taken to the American lines. The carriages were left in the gun-house for General Gage.

With the same secrecy and adroitness the Americans carried off the cannon from the battery at Charlestown, under the guns of the men-of-war. They are working like beavers to collect warlike stores at Watertown, Concord, and Worcester. Thousands of bullets and thousands of cartridges are sent out by the Bostonians, concealed under loads of manure.

Boston is now crowded with troops and with Tory refugees from the country. Winter is coming, and the general must get his soldiers under cover. He must have barracks. But to have barracks he must first have lumber and bricks, and next he must have laborers to build them. The people will neither sell to him nor work for him. If they can freeze the soldiers out, so much the worse for the soldiers. So for some time longer, and far into the winter, the red-coats shiver in their tents, and curse the Yankees who are the cause. Many sicken, many run away, and not a few die and are buried at the foot of the Common.[1]

[1] Their bones now moulder there, in the burial-ground enclosed at the angle formed by Boylston and Charles Streets.

A GARRISONED TOWN. 115

As we are still in the neighborhood of the Common, let us see what is going on there. To-day a deserter who has been caught is to suffer the sentence of a court-martial. It is a cruel sentence. He is to be shot to death. In the presence of the whole army the unfortunate is taken to the place of execution, at the foot of the Common, and after being blindfolded and pinioned, and after receiving the prayers of the chaplain, is pierced with balls. His lifeless body is then stretched bleeding upon a coffin, while the whole army marches past.

Every fine day the troops are drilled and exercised in firing at a target. When they begin shooting Yankees they mean to do execution. A big target is placed in the river at the foot of the Common at which they fire. One day a countryman who had strayed to this place stood by, laughing heartily to see a whole regiment fire at the target without hitting it. This made the soldiers angry.

"What are you laughing at, sirrah?" exclaimed the officer in command.

"You'll be mad if I tell, gineral," drawled the rustic.

"No; speak out."

"Why then, curnel, I laugh to see them fire so blamed awkward. Why, I'll be bound I hit that mark ten times running."

"Ah! will you? We shall see. Here, corporal, bring five of the best guns, and load them for this honest man."

"You need n't bring so many, major; one's a plenty.

Haw! haw! Give me the first that's handy. But all the same to yew, capting, I choose to load it myself."

He accordingly loaded, and having done so, asked the officer, "Wa'al, naow, lootenant, where shall I shoot?"

"To the right."

Bang went the piece. The soldiers ran up. The ball pierced the target to the right of the bull's-eye. The officer, amazed, declared the Yankee could not do it again. It was a chance shot, he said. The countryman chuckled to himself and again charged his gun.

"Where shall I fire?"

"To the left."

The countryman drove his bullet in the exact spot.

"Come! once more," urged the officer.

"Where naow?" asked the cool fellow.

"In the centre."

The third bullet struck exactly in the centre of the target. The soldiers stood aghast, and well they might. If this awkward, ungainly fellow in homespun had been shooting at them and they at him, he would have killed a man at every shot. But shooting at men *is* different from shooting at a mark.

"Why, sargunt," said the marksman, "I've got a boy tew hum that will toss up an apple and shoot out the seeds as it comes down."

We now begin to hear of Haldimand, of Pigot, of Prescott, Howe, Clinton, and Burgoyne. The levees at the

Province House grow more frequent and more brilliant. The bands give concerts and the officers' balls at Concert Hall which the Tory gentry only will attend. Faneuil Hall is to be turned into a theatre, and General Burgoyne has graciously promised to write a play taking off the Yankees. A play indeed! There will be one of another kind presently.

The officers at first live sumptuously on the fat of the land. Gold has no smell, and the country people who bring chickens and geese and turkeys, fresh eggs and butter and vegetables, into town are glad enough to get it.

These same officers also get, from the ships that arrive, turtles and pineapples and wine, and many a good thing besides. A jolly time over their mess-tables they have, giving each other dinners, drinking the healths of the pretty Boston girls, cracking jokes, and sneering at the Yankee *heroes*, as they contemptuously call them.

Captain Harris of the 5th falls over head and ears in love with a Miss Coffin and facetiously says he has found a coffin for his heart. So between balls, dinners, and reviews they idle away the time. "If 'Tommy' would only give us a chance at these insolent vagabonds!" they exclaim, "if he only would!"

X.

FANEUIL HALL AND THE NEIGHBORHOOD.

WELL, "Tommy" did at last give them a chance. On the 19th of April, 1775, he very secretly, as he thought, sent off a battalion of seven or eight hundred picked men to destroy the warlike stores the Americans had collected at Concord. While they are on the way let us look over the North End of the town, the most seditious and turbulent portion of it.

Choosing for our starting-point the Brattle Street Church,[1] in which Doctor Cooper vigorously preaches liberty up and prays tyranny down, and in which John Hancock goes to meeting, we speedily get into the region known as Dock Square, from the fact that the oldest landing-place, now widened, and skirted by wharves, is here.

We are facing the water-side. At our left, forming an angle, the old building shown in the first chapter has a

[1] This building was taken down several years ago to make way for the splendid block of stores now on the same site. It stood facing up Brattle Street, occupying the corner and angle made by Brattle Square.

special quaintness of its own. It is nicknamed The Old Cocked Hat. Even now it is getting out of date, and looks queerly, with its diminutive windows and its front

BRATTLE STREET CHURCH.

covered over with coarse plaster in which gravel and broken glass are mixed, and in which we see the year of its erection — 1680.

But a larger and far more imposing structure at the right attracts our attention. We are before Faneuil Hall, only the town market-house, yet a building destined, if such a thing can be said of a pile of brick and mortar, to make a noise in the world. From the centre of the roof rises a lofty tower, and on the summit of the tower a gilded grasshopper does duty as a weather-vane.

CANNON-BALL IN THE WINDOW.[1]

Some people think this grasshopper is there because it was the old Athenian symbol. But it is not so. The Athenians, it is true, reverenced this insect, which, like man, came forth from the earth itself, and so was typical of him. But the fact probably is that when Peter Faneuil,[2] who so generously gave the hall to the town, and who was a rich merchant, came to consult with the architect, the Royal Exchange of London was taken for a model. The founder of this building, Sir Thomas Gresham, had mounted a grasshopper upon it, and Smybert, the architect of Faneuil Hall, an Englishman, and a painter of some note, too, very likely had this in mind.

The open space around Faneuil Hall is used as a market-place, and the railings are conveniently there for the country-people to hitch their horses to when they come in with their produce, or for the people of the town to tie

[1] The engraving shows a cannon-ball that struck the wall when Washington opened his batteries on the town.

[2] Always pronounced "Funnel," even within the writer's remembrance, by old people.

their nags to when they come to town-meeting; for this is now also the town-house in consequence of the Court House in King Street having long been too small to accom-

FANEUIL HALL.

modate courts, and legislatures, and town officials, together. But Faneuil built this house, and gave it to the town to be used as a market and for holding town-meetings. It was a very munificent gift. And thus the town-meetings, beginning here in this period of great political excitement, will give immortality to the name of Faneuil Hall.[1]

[1] During the siege the British garrison relieved the monotony of the winter by turning Faneuil Hall into a theatre, in which they had concerts and plays twice a week, the performers being officers assisted by their lady friends. One night, while a farce by General Burgoyne, called the Blockade of Boston, was being acted, the Americans made

The fire of January 13, 1763, destroyed the whole interior, but the town promptly voted to rebuild, and the

province government at once authorized the town to raise funds to do this by a lottery.[1] No time was lost. In March the house was again ready for public business, and

a sortie and set fire to several houses in Charlestown that had escaped the general conflagration and were now occupied by the enemy. A tremendous firing immediately began from the redoubts on Bunker Hill, where everything was in confusion. Hearing this uproar, the sentry stationed at the door of the play-house rushed upon the stage, vociferating, " Turn out ! turn out ! They 're hard at it, hammer and tongs." The audience, supposing the sergeant was acting a part, loudly applauded, and it was some time before the amazed fellow could be heard. When he could he shouted, " What the d—— are ye all about ! If ye won't belave me, be St. Patrick ye need only go to the door, and there ye 'll hear and see both."

The audience immediately rose in consternation. They had not calculated upon the Americans taking so prominent a part.

[1] Lotteries are now prohibited, but no one then thought them vicious, and people who would not *give* a penny would take the chance of gaining a prize.

at a meeting to celebrate the event it was again dedicated in an eloquent speech by James Otis, the most eloquent Bostonian of his day.

We have said a good deal about the English soldiery. As Faneuil Hall became the rendezvous of the citizen soldiery, let us briefly review them, and see how they compare with regulars.

The Common was their training-ground, recollect, from the time of the first Puritan muster.

By the side of the well-uniformed British regulars our militia, we fear, had formerly made a very mean appearance. But with the growth of a military spirit they began to emulate them, — to pay attention to their own discipline, their dress, their arms.

The companies of the Boston or Suffolk Regiment were all uniformed in blue, each company having its drummers and fifers dressed in white. The regiment also had a company of grenadiers, dressed in red, the same as the British regiments had. It had also a band of music, of eight pieces, that was thought by the partial Bostonians to perform as well as the British bands.

There was also the Cadet Company, the crack corps of them all, having its own band. It was commanded by Colonel John Hancock; but when General Gage began to put his master's tyrannous edicts in force he dismissed Colonel Hancock, and so the company indignantly voted to disband, and sent their colors to the general in token that they would no more be foot-guards of his. For they were a kind of privileged corps, and were called the Governor's Guards.

Then there was Paddock's company of artillery, with four field-pieces. And there was also the Ancient and Honorable Artillery Company, the oldest military organization in the whole country, going way back to the Puritan times, and having special field-days of its own. This was also a well-uniformed and well-disciplined body of men, the same as the others.[1] Why, some of its commanders had fought with the great Cromwell, and had helped to make and unmake kings. Old eyes and young eyes sparkled when the drums of the Ancients, beating from street to street, called the company to assemble for parade.

But now their old training-ground, the Common, is in possession of the British troops. They are prohibited from entering it. Still, they are determined to parade, as usual, on their annual field-day. They turn out with full ranks and march to Copp's Hill, into a piece of ground of which they are the owners.

The British frigate Lively is moored in the ferry-way, — we know for what purpose. As the Ancients march proudly up the hill, in full view, the boatswain's whistle pipes its shrill call, "All hands on deck!" The ports fly

---

[1] We hope to see a revival of its old traditions in this distinguished corps, at no distant day.

open and the guns are run out. The jack-tars run to the
guns. The marines man the quarter-deck and scramble
hastily up into the round tops. They think the Yankees
are surely coming to exchange compliments with them in
their own kind — powder and ball, shot and shell. What

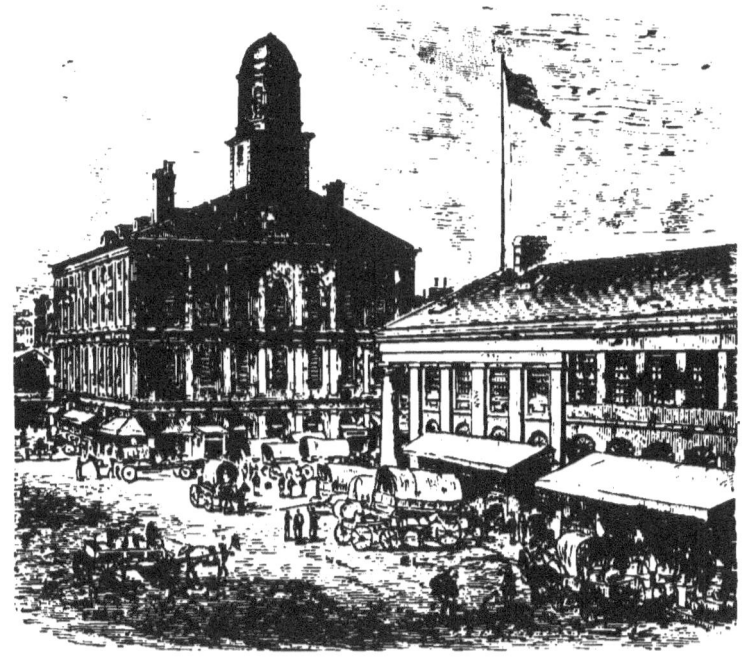

NEW FANEUIL HALL.

a jolly fright they are in at this apparition of only fifty
Ancients in arms! And how these audacious rebels
split their sides laughing!

The commander of the Ancients was asked, —

"What would you have done if a body of British troops

had opposed your entrance to Copp's Hill, as they had opposed your marching into the Common?"

"I would have given the order to 'Fix bayonets.'"

"Well, what then?"

"I would have ordered my men to charge; and I would have forced my way at the point of the bayonet, as surely as I would into my own house if it were in possession of a gang of thieves."

Well answered, gallant Captain Bell. Talk about the "King's Own"! This martial band is the "People's Own."

So we see that the boys in blue are not a bit afraid of the boys in red. But we shudder, all the same, to think how soon they will cross bayonets on the field of battle.

To return to Faneuil Hall. Well, when the Bostonians were ordered to surrender their arms, they came here, very sorrowfully, to hand them over to the officer appointed by General Gage.

But we cannot loiter. We must on to other scenes. Let us then turn to the left and walk through Union Street, stopping before we reach Hanover to look at Boston Stone.[1] The stones,

[1] This is now seen solidly imbedded in the rear wall of the building fronting Hanover Street, but approached at the back from Marshall's Lane.

for there are two, consist of a globe, and an oblong block, with a cavity into which the globe exactly fits. They were originally used for grinding paint, but came, in time, to be spoken of as Boston Stone, from the famous London Stone in Cannon Street.

In a very ancient English poem by John Lydgate, he says: —

> "Then went I forth by London Stone,
>   Throughout all Canwick Street;
> Drapers much cloth me offered anon;
>   Then comes me one cried hot sheep's feet;
> One cried mackerel, rushes green, another gave greet;
>   One bade me buy a hood to cover my head;
> But for want of money I might not be sped."[1]

Were we to look in at the shop-window of an old brick building making the turning from Union Street into Marshall's Lane we should probably see a young man of two and twenty, or thereabouts, either waiting upon, or waiting for a customer to walk into the shop. His name? Benjamin Thompson. Not a very high-sounding one, to be sure; but when you learn that he afterwards took that of Count Rumford, the case is altered.[2]

Not forgetting that Franklin's father lived at the upper corner of Union Street, we will cross over Hanover toward

---

[1] See also Jack Cade, Act IV., Scene VI.

[2] The old building, occupied as an oyster-house, is still standing. You can easily learn something about this very eminent personage that I have not room to tell.

the Mill Pond, in which the boy Franklin sailed his chip boats.

The boy Benjamin Franklin has already fought and won his way to places of high honor, notwithstanding his parents were very poor, humble people. Let him tell us how he gained an education in his own words.

When Franklin returned from England — he was then a very young man — the captain of the vessel in which he had come put a note into his hands. Ben opened it and read : —

"G. Burnet's compliments await young Mr. Franklin, and should be glad of half an hour's chat with him over a glass of wine."

"G. Burnet," said Ben aloud. "Who is G. Burnet?"

"Why," replied the captain, with a smile at Ben's puzzled looks, "'t is the governor himself wishes to see you; no other."

So to the governor's Ben went. After astounding His Excellency with the extent of his information the governor asked him, —

"Well, and pray at what college did you study Locke on the Understanding, at thirteen?"

"Why, sir, it was my misfortune never to be at a college, nor even at a grammar school, except nine months."

Here the governor sprang from his seat, and, staring at Ben, cried out, "The deuce! Well, where then — where did you get your education, pray?"

GREEN DRAGON TAVERN.

"At home, sir. In a tallow-chandler's shop."

"In a *tallow-chandler's* shop?" screamed the governor.

"Yes, sir. My father was a poor old tallow-chandler, with sixteen children, and I the youngest of all. At eight he put me to school, but, finding he could not spare the money from the rest of the children to keep me there, he took me home into the shop, where I assisted him by twisting candle-wicks and filling the moulds all day, and at night I read by myself. At twelve my father bound me to my brother, a printer, in Boston. With him I worked hard all day at the press and the cases, and again read by myself at night."

SIGN OF THE GREEN DRAGON.

The governor could not believe this story until he asked the captain, who confirmed every word of it.

Here on the west side of Union Street is a two-story

brick house. From the front projects an iron rod, on which crouches a dragon, of copper. The house is certainly a tavern. Yes, it is the already famous Green Dragon.[1]

But first let us briefly refer to the custom of celebrating the anniversary of the Gunpowder Plot,[2] which is here called Pope Day. Young Boston is as loyal and fully as boisterous as Young London, which has its orgie, too, finished by burning the Pope at Temple Bar as the Boston Pope is on Copp's Hill. The occasion served a double purpose, because it afforded a coveted opportunity for North End and South End to have a pitched battle in the streets. We do not know how this strange animosity between these two sections of the town may have originated, but it was a very bitter and determined one until the Revolution gave both parties a worthier object for their surplus pugnacity. But until then a South End boy hardly dared show his head in the North End; and *vice versa*, a North End boy would think twice before venturing into the enemy's territory. Such was the feeling of the sections.[3]

---

[1] Though the original building is gone the site is easily identified by the tablet in the wall of the present one, having a dragon sculptured upon it.

[2] Your English History will tell what this was.

[3] This unaccountable animosity quite lately existed, as the writer knows from experience, between the boys of the North End and the Charlestown boys. It even included young men.

On Pope Day each section had its own procession, each being pretty sure to encounter the other in its route; and when the rivals did meet, a battle with fists, stones, and sticks ensued to see which could capture the other's Pope, or Pageant, as it was called. The North End Pope was never, it is said, taken but once.

Some planks were laid on wheels, on which was placed an effigy of the Pope, with the devil at his elbow, both being dressed to look as hideous as possible. After parading through the principal streets a bonfire was built in which the mock Pope, and strange to say, the devil too, were burnt to a cinder. You see, altogether, what was first intended perhaps to be a very patriotic, grew to be a very foolish and disgraceful, affair. But we are relating, not excusing it. It was a custom.

Once, it is said, when the clumsy carriage of the South End Pope broke down, young Harry Knox, in order to prevent the disgrace which would surely follow its capture, putting his own muscular shoulder in the place of the broken wheel, bore the vehicle off in triumph, amid the yells and jeers of the combatants.

The Green Dragon was the muster-place of the North Enders for this mock parade. But something far more serious is now going on there.

Now, while General Gage and his officers are deliberating, planning, and working at the Province House how to forge their fetters more and more strongly, counter-plotting is going on, and treason hatching in the Green Dragon by the patriotic mechanics of this part of the town. These men were the muscle of the Revolution. Joseph Warren, a young physician, was their adored leader. He chose Paul Revere to be his right-hand man, for his daring, his prudence, and his decision of character.

It is their object to learn what General Gage means to do, and if possible to frustrate it. For this purpose they hold secret meetings, to which no one is admitted until he takes a solemn oath on the Bible not to reveal anything that may be said or done except to such well-known and trusted leaders as Samuel Adams, Hancock, or Warren. But a traitor is among them, although they do not know it.

A hundred eyes narrowly watch the soldiers, night and day. Spies are even in the Province House itself. They expect and are intently watching for some hostile act. They are a Vigilance Committee, — all eyes and ears, but close as the tomb.

So, General Gage, you had hardly given the order for the grenadiers and light infantry of the army to march to Concord, before it was known to these men, who are sworn to defeat your plans.

And they are fully as determined, and much more confident in the righteousness of their cause, than yourself.

All this time the Massachusetts Provincial Congress, sitting at Cambridge, or Watertown, is organizing its army. They mean that King George III., Lord North, and General Gage, their weapon, shall understand that when it comes to "crushing out," two can play at that game. Already Gage has blustered and threatened, already they have been called "traitors" and "rebels"; still they are no less determined. Hard words are nothing to the hard knocks that are coming. All they ask is that their friends in Boston will not let the soldiers steal a march upon them. We shall see that those friends will not fail. They are true as steel. Great Britain *is* great, but the spirit of liberty is far greater. For this will men do and dare everything.

Cunning general! He relieved from duty, several days ago, the soldiers he meant to send out to destroy the stores at Concord. The soldiers knew at once that this meant there was *something else* in the wind besides mounting guard and drilling. The inhabitants knew it as well as they. It was their notice to be more watchful than ever. They redoubled their vigilance. Crafty General Gage! A pretty mess you have made of it, to be sure.

At any rate, on Saturday, April 16, the very day following the order not to put the grenadiers and light infantry on duty, Warren sent his trusty Revere with a message to Hancock and Adams, who were then at Lexington. While on his way back, Revere planned with some friends in Charlestown how to give them intelligence of troops marching into the country. This was necessary, for every avenue was now so strictly guarded that he did not feel sure a messenger would be able to get out of the town with the news.

Opposite to where they stood, lifted high above Copp's Hill, was the steeple of the North Episcopal, or Christ Church.

"If the British go out by water, we will show two lanterns in yonder tower; and if by land, one," said Revere to his friends.

"Agreed, and we will watch the ferry here, while our friends watch Roxbury side. If the British get out without our knowing it, they will catch a weasel asleep, that's all."

"Good!" Paul Revere then returned across the river to give an account of his doings to Dr. Warren.

Although the town was getting too hot to hold such as he, yet, because convinced that he could better serve the patriot cause by remaining in Boston, he did so.

On Tuesday evening, the 18th, at the hour fixed upon, the soldiers, leaving their barracks, marched silently to the rendezvous at the foot of the Common. It is clear as day that the long-expected blow is going to fall.

Of course these troops did not march unseen. The inhabitants saw them; and what is more, they guessed where they were going and what was their errand. They gathered in little knots in the streets, and very earnestly discussed the danger their friends were in.

With his pickets on the Neck, his guards at the ferry,

and his watches on board the men-of-war, General Gage thinks Boston is a trap of which he alone holds the key.

But at ten o'clock at night, after the troops had set out, Earl Percy, coming from the Province House, where he had been closeted with his general, ran across these groups of the townspeople conversing with great animation. One said, loud enough for the earl to hear: —

"The British troops have marched, but will miss their aim."

"What aim?" asked the earl, very much surprised.

"The cannon at Concord," was the reply.

Lord Percy instantly turned on his heel, and went back to tell General Gage what he had heard.

"Ah!" exclaimed the amazed chief, "I have been betrayed!"

No, General, you are only outwitted.

With the cannon and stores at Concord, and the troops in Boston, it was really no difficult matter for the Bostonians to put this and that together, even if nobody had let the cat out of the bag.

At ten o'clock Warren sent in haste for Revere. Revere must ride to Lexington, post-haste, see Hancock and Adams, and warn them to be on their guard. Of course, the British column, on its march, must pass through Lexington.

Revere hurries off to get ready. But, as he may not be able to give the guards the slip, he thinks of the signal agreed upon. He first sees a friend whom he can trust, and gets him to make the signal. Then he picks up two more friends, and together they glide like shadows down the grass-grown wharf, draw a canoe from its hiding-place, and with muffled oars push out upon the dark river, over which the rising moon is just beginning to shed a pale lustre, and over which the huge black hulks of the ships of war rise threateningly. Their hearts beat quickly as they pass within hail. All's safe. They pass unseen, and in a few moments more land.

"We have seen your signals," exclaimed the watchers. "Look there!"

And there, sure enough, from the dusky steeple the two warning lights shone out bright and clear. Now for Lexington. They bring Revere a beast of good mettle. He leaps into the saddle, puts spurs to his horse, and darkness closes around him. The steed with eyes of flame, sparks flying from his iron hoofs, his belly to the ground, the rider with pinched lips, eyes piercing the night, and bent eagerly over the saddle-bow, as if his own impatience outran that of his flying courser, are incarnate messengers of war. The pickets set to stop him he leaves behind. Then away again! "Up and arm!" he shouts. "Up and arm!" echoes through the silent village-streets, affrighting the startled yeomen from their slumbers. "Up and arm!" comes faintly back, as rider and steed vanish out of sight. Shout, Revere! The hour is come. Your voice is the signal for war. Ride hard! life and death are in your speed.

And as the regulars march along in the cool of the morning, to the right, to the left, in front, they hear the clang of alarm-bells and the noise of gunshots. In the houses, which look silent as the tomb, men are hurriedly buckling on weapons, snatching a mouthful of food, or whispering hasty farewells. The women are pale, but helpful and resolute. The crisis has indeed come. All Middlesex is up in arms.

What a simple-minded old gentleman you are, General Gage, to be sure!

XI.

THE OLD NORTH END.

INSTEAD of keeping on down Middle Street, as the lower end of Hanover Street is called, we now cross the Mill Creek by a bridge, and, turning to the left, take our way through Back or Salem Street.

This Mill Creek, as we see from the bridge, is a narrow water-course, connecting the Mill Pond at our left with the harbor at our right. Boats pass through it.

In a few minutes the ground begins to ascend. Rising in front of us is the high tower and pointed steeple of Christ Church, — the church which has played so important a part in the march to Lexington and Concord.[1]

---

[1] Inserted in the masonry of the tower-front is a tablet with this inscription: —

THE SIGNAL LANTERNS OF
PAUL REVERE,
DISPLAYED IN THE STEEPLE OF THIS CHURCH,
APRIL 18, 1775,
WARNED THE COUNTRY OF THE MARCH
OF THE BRITISH TROOPS
TO LEXINGTON AND CONCORD.

As we walk along, many of the houses are occupied by British officers, who have hired them, or — unfrequently, we think, for here the people are true blue, almost to a man — have obtained lodgings with the family. We see them going in and out. We see them at the windows, nodding and saluting their brother officers who are passing along the street. Those in the street are ogling the girls at the windows.

CHRIST CHURCH.

And now and then, noticing a sentinel pacing before a door, we know it to be the residence of some officer of rank. Seeing how the neighborhood is thus crowded with redcoats, we are amazed at the boldness of giving signals from this steeple, and cannot refuse our admiration for the act.

But now, as we approach nearer to the church, a silvery chime breaks forth from the tower. List to the sweet clamor of the bells! Ding, dong, ding! There is music in the air. We stop and listen to these iron tongues and these brazen throats loudly singing the old, old hymns. Though it reminds us of it, this church-tower is far better than the heathen statue in which music was concealed. Thirty years ago, one Christmas morn, these bells rang out their first peal. Long may their tuneful echoes be wafted by the breeze above the house-tops of the living and the dead!

Yet, for all this, some of the common people, who do not like the Episcopal Church one bit more than their Puritan ancestors did, shake their heads when they hear the chimes. They tell us, and really believe too, that these bells were blessed by the Pope of Rome, and have, therefore, power to dispel evil spirits. These are old wives' tales, you will say. No, they are relics of a superstition, dying very slowly, but dying.

Let us enter. A cool light comes in through the windows, dimly illuminating the interior. We feel awed and subdued, because it is a temple consecrated to the Deity. Everything is stiff, stately, and formal. The pews are high, straight-backed, and as uncomfortable as can be. The pulpit-base is a gilded cluster of feathers, resembling a Corinthian capital. The chandeliers hanging from the vaulted roof, and those little images of saints decorating the organ-loft, are trophies of war, taken from a French vessel that was carrying them to some cathedral in a foreign land. The Bible and prayer-book, the communion vessels of silver, are gifts of his most gracious majesty, George II., whose monogram adorns them. Now the organ peals; the rector, clad in his immaculate white surplice and his bands, advancing to the sacred desk, begins the service.

This clergyman is still young. He is the son of the Rev. Mather Byles, whom we have already visited. When he prays for the king and the royal family, it is with such earnestness that we at once know him for a Loyalist. Perhaps there is a tremor in his voice, for blood has flowed all along the road to Lexington and Concord. Well may his voice falter a little.[1]

From Christ Church we will wend our way first to the top of Copp's Hill, which is in part occupied by one of our most ancient cemeteries. Let us take this street turning to the left, Hull Street. In this old ground, covered with a heavy slab of freestone, which years have rounded

[1] It was the common custom to inter under the old churches. The body of Major Pitcairn, killed at Bunker Hill, was placed in a vault here. On the fly-leaf of a prayer-book, used in this church, I once read, "Major Pitcairn's compliments to the gentleman overhead, and begs he will not snore so loud, as he disturbs his slumbers."

Janson, an English traveller, says he went down into the crypt beneath the church. He saw there the skeletons of a number of British officers who fell at Bunker Hill. They were not in coffins, but piled one upon another, with their faded regimentals hanging in tatters about them.

at the edges, is the tomb of the Mathers, Increase and Cotton, father and son, who, during their lives, were distinguished for learning, piety, and usefulness, above most of the men of their day and generation. And these two men are a part of the times in which they lived, and with which they had so much to do. In their day no two men were more revered. None will live longer in our history. Around them moulder the bones of many generations.[1]

TOMB OF THE MATHERS.

This hill is the playground of the North End boys. It is also the promenade of the older people, who delight to

[1] This tomb, which is always the first visited, marks the central portion of the old, original burying-place, now much enlarged by successive additions. In the slab covering the vault a square of slate is inserted, on which is cut: —

"REVEREND DRS. INCREASE, COTTON, AND SAMUEL MATHER WERE INTERRED IN THIS VAULT.

'T IS THE TOMB OF OUR FATHERS MATHER. — CROCKERS.

    I. DIED AUG. 27, 1723. Æt 84.
    C. DIED FEB. 13, 1727. Æt 65.
    S. DIED JUNE 27, 1785. Æt 79."

Samuel, the last named, was the son of Cotton.

Among the thickset stones we can pick out those first used to mark a grave. They are mere boulders taken from the seashore, and roughly cut on one surface with the name, age, and date of the deceased person. Of this kind is the stone of Nicholas Upshall, the Quaker tavern-keeper of the North End.

walk here in the cool of the evening, when the sea-breeze fans the heated air. Here ended the Pope Day celebrations with bonfires and huzzas. And from here, in plain view, rise the green heights of Charlestown, with the town and shipping at their feet.

Looking down upon the shining surface of the river, a warlike ship, brave with flags, swings slowly with the tide. Boats are passing between the shores under the guns of this ship. On whatever side we turn, we see the town threatened by cannon. And to think that the word of one man can drench all this fair scene in blood!

THE GLASGOW.

Hull Street, which conducted us to the cemetery, is so named for John Hull, who coined the silver money for the colony so long ago. It is one of the old-time stories that when his daughter Judith married, she received her own weight in silver shillings for a wedding portion. So she was worth her weight in silver at least. Copp is a family name. We read it on the gravestones, bent with age.

But this eminence is now put to other uses than for the burial of the dead. The northern end, fronting Charlestown, is disfigured by an earthwork newly thrown up,

THE OLD NORTH END.   145

from which the muzzles of cannon threaten the opposite shore. This battery is that of the Royal Artillery. These guns are destined to play a part in the near future.[1]

We cannot delay here, for events hasten, and so must we. Descending from the hill-top to the side opposite that by which we entered, Charter Street conducts us toward the water-side, into a region full of the flavor of the sea. This street takes its name from the new charter granted by King William III.; and only a little way down, at the corner of Salem Street, is the residence of Sir William Phips, who was the first governor under this charter. So the name, like Union, really means something.

A word about this governor and his really fine brick mansion, which stands in the midst of a garden running two hundred feet back up the hill, and for more than half that distance on Salem Street, with outhouses for the servants and stables for the horses.

He was a poor boy who, by energy and perseverance, won his way to the proud position of governor in the face of many obstacles. The king knighted him for recovering the treasure of a galleon of which £16,000 fell to his share. So that he found himself all at once both famous and rich.

This poor boy had dreamed that he would become rich enough to build him a house on the Green Lane, as this

[1] The stone of Captain Daniel Malcom bears the mark of bullets, fired perhaps in mere wantonness by the soldiers.

part of Salem Street was once called. We have seen that he lived to realize his dream.

The governor's Christian name was William, the same as the king's, and his wife's was Mary, the same as the Queen's. Of course all the public acts of the governor were issued in the name of William and Mary. It is said that once, when the governor was absent from home, his wife was entreated to use her influence with her husband in behalf of a poor woman who was lying in jail on a charge of witchcraft. The good lady was so affected by the tale that she took a piece of paper and made out an order on the spot for the poor woman's release. And what did she do but sign it "William and Mary"! This was high treason, to sign the names of their majesties, the king and queen; but it passed for a joke, which the old people loved to tell with infinite relish at the expense of William and Mary Phips.

Let us turn into this narrow lane — Henchman's Lane — which will take us directly to the shore, and among the shipyards.

After Governor Phips's time his house was owned by a Captain Gruchy, — the same man who gave the chandeliers to Christ Church. He was a native of the island of Jersey and also owned all the land running from his house to the water-side. People lift their eyebrows a little when they hear his name mentioned. Perhaps they mean that this Captain Gruchy was a bit of a free-trader.

THE OLD NORTH END. 147

Perhaps it is only the gossip of the time that gives him this character.

But when England and France were at war, in '45, Gruchy's vessels, armed to the teeth, pounced upon any stray "Mounseer" they found skulking along the Spanish Main. The prize vessels were sent to Boston and sold, or if worthless sunk at sea. Captain Gruchy sunk three to make himself a wharf at the North End. But the rich silks, the spices and wines, the silver piastres and golden doubloons, were disposed of in a more mysterious way. The privateering merchant built an underground arch of brick, leading all the way from his house down to the beach; and on the first dark night after a vessel dropped anchor, his boats, loaded with valuable booty, pulled with muffled oars to the shore, where the goods were taken by the sailors up to the captain's house through the arch, lighted by flaring torches. The mouth of the arch, which was large enough for boats to enter, was concealed by a wharf running out into the river. And so the king was cheated of his share. [1]

---

[1] This arch was long a puzzle to the few who knew of its existence. Their idea was that it was the retreat of pirates, in which they could lie concealed or hide their goods. But while writing Landmarks of Boston I found an account of it in a manuscript which may be read on pages 199, 200 of that book. A subterranean arch, such as was often constructed in the old times for concealing contraband goods, may be still seen in the cellar of Mr. Nolan's house, on Charter Street, near the cemetery. This may be identical with the arch of Captain Gruchy.

Continuing our ramble by the shore we are in the region exclusively devoted to shipwrights, boatbuilders, mast-makers, and the smell of pitch and oakum. This is also Jack's favorite haunt, as we know by frequent tippling-houses, out of which he comes with rolling gait and a very red face. Many of these jolly tars are man-of-war's men, who have come on shore for a lark. The women are generally coarse, ill-featured, and bold. The children, of whom there are enough and to spare, look dirty and squalid. This region is the Wapping of Boston. Notice the narrow lanes, the crooked alleys, the crazy rookeries topped by clothes-lines and huge chimneys. Hark to the calker's mallets, the "Yo heave ho!" "Cheerily, lads!" of the crews getting up their anchors, the boatswain's whistle and stroke of the bell on board the men-of-war, calling away a boat's crew or tolling the hour! See the spars, tall and tapering, around which long pennants cling like painted serpents! Yes, this is the Old North End.

But this activity is of war, not peace.

We are now come through Lynn Street, which here skirts the water as far as the North Battery.[1] This North Battery was built to protect the town from foreign foes, but General Gage has now seized and dismantled it. This was the way it was done.

Two war-ships were anchored near by in the stream, with springs on their cables, all ready for an engagement,

---

[1] Shown in Revere's Picture of Boston on p. 79.

while a party of soldiers went to work spiking the guns; for the general feared that the "rascally Bostonians" might carry these great guns off, as they had previously done the "little barkers" from the gun-house. All this was very secretly effected under cover of the night.

But the affair was not to end thus. After the soldiers had finished spiking the cannon, two naval officers took it into their heads to go and see if the work was properly done. The woman who had charge of the keys unlocked the gate and let them in; but no sooner were they fairly inside, than she turned the key, locking them up. The walls were too high for them to climb, and the tide was too low for them to drop from the port-holes. So there they remained, shouting to be taken off, while the crowd, running up at the cries, treated the imprisoned Britons to cutting remarks and ironical laughter still more cutting.

We will now turn away from the water, its sights and sounds, and taking this narrow lane, opening a long crack among the maze of wooden houses, reach a spot of historic ground in which we can profitably spend a quarter of an hour.

We have at last come to North Square, which is an open space, in form like a triangle, and so narrow at its entrance, where the point is, that only a single vehicle can pass at a time. At the head of this space, and facing it, stands the old Second Church of Boston, — the church of the Mathers. It is a wooden building, with low, square tower; yet humble as it looks, no house of worship in all the colonies can rival its history. The words spoken

THE OLD HOUSE IN SHIP (NORTH) STREET.

from its pulpit passed from lip to lip as the sacred oracles of the olden time. In those days the voice of the preacher was as the voice of God.

Some of the houses here are already hallowed by age. Moss covers the roofs. The great chimney-stacks show wide cracks made by earthquakes, sent, as the people believed, to destroy them in their sin. Yet there are others which seem looking scornfully down, in their pride, upon their humble neighbors.

This one at the corner of the alley is the late residence of Sir Charles Frankland, knight, whose adventures read like

FRANKLAND'S HOUSE.

a tale of romance.[1] It was built by the rich merchant, William Clark, who is buried on Copp's Hill, and from whom this vacant space was called Clark's Square.

But next to the baronet's, in Garden Court, is another fine house, — the one to which we promised to bring you,

---

[1] He was crushed by the terrible earthquake at Lisbon, and rescued by his lady-love, Agnes, whom the poet Holmes has immortalized.

not long ago. In this stately mansion, with its pilasters, and its balconied entrance, resided the man whom the Bostonians hate so bitterly that his very name is greeted with hisses when spoken in a public assemblage. It is the house of Thomas Hutchinson, the man who has had so much to do in bringing about the crisis through which we are now passing.

THE HUTCHINSON MANSION.

A Boston boy, yet false to the land of his birth! Yes, it must so go down in history. Of the old Puritan stock, of the lineage of those who suffered for greater liberty of thought and speech in the old days, Thomas Hutchinson placed himself on the side of oppression when his own countrymen were the oppressed. There he must remain. He was able and learned, but he was also grasping and ambitious. He was a man of exemplary private character, but a scheming and unscrupulous politician. He possessed an amiable disposition. As a citizen he was respected, while as a public man he was detested. We do not think he was generous, for the people nicknamed him "Stingy Tommy," and the people never make a mistake in their estimate of a man.

During the Stamp Act troubles a mob attacked and gutted this house. In its blind fury it destroyed not only rich furniture and costly ornaments, but scattered his valuable library in the streets and his manuscripts to the four winds. The lieutenant-governor and his family fled in great fear, and hid themselves in the neighborhood until the rioters had dispersed. They then crept back to their plundered and desolate abode. This was certainly a cruel and a wanton act. All good people regretted it. But the mob is a wild animal goaded to madness.

The king having need of a military man, General Gage received his command to be governor, and Hutchinson, disappointed, perhaps, at not securing the vacant position, has sailed for England, never to return. There we will leave him.

Farther down the square is the house of that bold Liberty Boy, Paul Revere.[1] A little farther on we come

---

[1] This house, a wooden one, with the upper story overhanging, is still standing. The next, now demolished, once belonged to the family of Commodore Downes.

to the lodgings of a soldier whose name is already written in letters of blood. Major Pitcairn lives here.

No corner of old Boston has more distinct traits than this, in which we now are. It is almost a community by itself. It has its own meeting-house, its costly mansions, its humble dwellings. It has its rich and poor, its shops, and even its own tavern. It is a centre from which a local influence spreads to a great distance. It is also full of its own traditions.

The family names are themselves curious. Here are Winter, Spring, Summer, and Fall; Frost, Snow, and Hale; Leg, Hart, and Head; Milk, Water, and Beer.

The wealthy and the titled are a law unto themselves, and their ways and privileges are respected. But when a citizen of humble calling and not over-much wit gives himself airs, the case is different. A tailor here took it into his head to erase the word "tailor" from his sign, putting that of "merchant" in its place. The next day the following lampoon was found nailed to his door-post: —

> "See *Merchant* Adams, reverend beau,
> With his high-heel shoes and Rocalow,
> With cocked-up hat and periwig,
> No man on earth struts forth so big.
> He 's left his goose to roast still more,
> And placed the merchant on his door."

When superstition was rife, nothing was too marvellous for belief. It was enough to whisper that such or such a person was a witch to insure his or her being regarded with fear and aversion. Old Mrs. Cary, who lived here, was a reputed witch. Rosemary being then considered a cure for the asthma was in demand for invalids suffering from this disease. At one time no rosemary could be had in the town for love or money. Suddenly it became noised about that Mother Cary had a great store of the herb. It was said and believed that she had made a trip to Bermuda and back in an egg-shell in a single night, to obtain the medicinal plant.

This cruel suspicion followed her to the grave, and beyond the grave. When she died the vault in which she was buried was permitted to lie open for many years, as the sepulchre of one not entitled to Christian burial.

Another old woman, Mother Hale, had nine cats, — the sorcerer's cabalistic number, — which she was in the habit of consulting to give information where stolen goods were secreted. No doubt she had many clients.

We have now finished our circuit of the old town. Without more delay, we must enter upon those scenes of war and bloodshed which are to make or mar the destinies of a proud and spirited people. God defend the right!

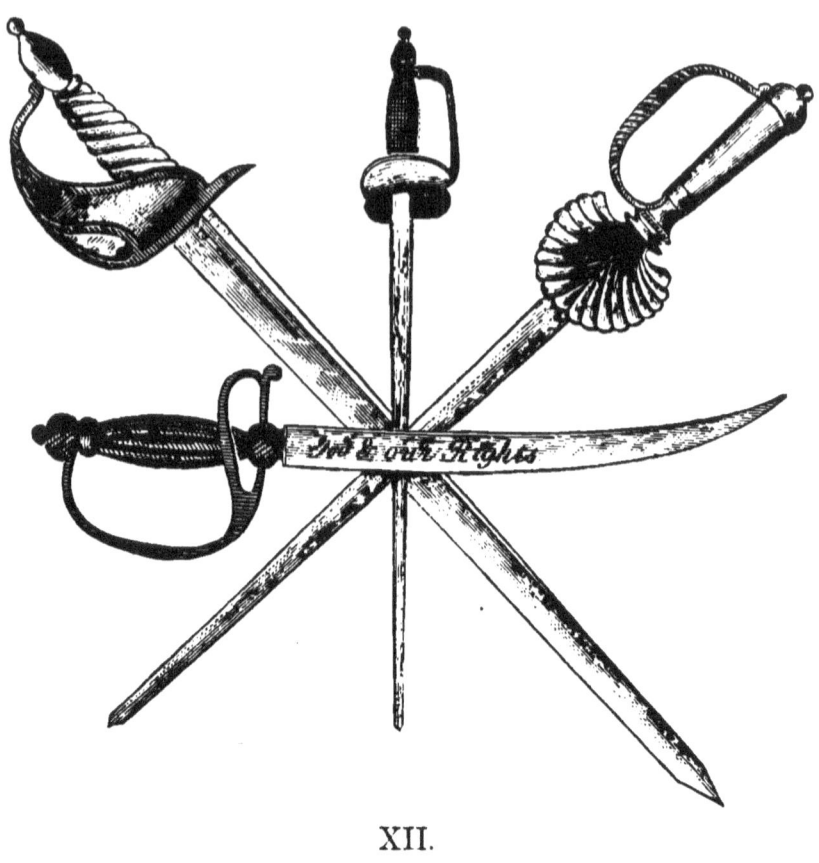

XII.

TO ARMS! TO ARMS![1]

WHILE in England they were saying of the provincials such cutting things as "It was romantic to think they would fight," and "There was more military prowess

---

[1] The upright sword in the centre is Warren's; the one to the left, Governor Brooks's; to the right is one used in the battle. That with the curved blade, and the motto "God and our Rights," is Putnam's.

in a militia drummer," these same despised yeomanry were chasing about two thousand of the king's troops from Concord to Lexington, and from Lexington to Charlestown.

The army officers tried to laugh it off, and spoke lightly of it as "our little fracas" and "the lark with the rebels." But they felt the disgrace all the same, and burned to retrieve the shame to their arms. What! British grenadiers running away before countrymen! The thought was maddening. But thus it was. Besides, there was the eternal record of blood. That was no laughing matter.

On their side, the Americans, pouring from every town and village and hamlet in New England, filled the highways with the tramp of armed men. "To arms! To arms!" was the cry. Everywhere drums beating, columns forming in warlike array. On, on they pressed, by scores, by fifties, and by thousands. All these streams flowed steadily to one point. That point is Cambridge. That collection of armed men, the army of independence.

Thus out of the blood that had crimsoned the plains of Lexington and Concord sprung, vigorous and vengeful, an armed host. Thus in an instant was scattered to the winds the silly prediction that a single British regiment could march, unopposed, from one end of the colonies to the other. And thus Americans, smarting under a long series of injuries, rushed to arms with a fierce exultation, and a firm belief in the triumph of a righteous cause.

Some had muskets, some fowling-pieces, some a sword

only, but all had one mind. At last they were going to fight for their rights. The story had spread over all New England like wildfire. Every heart leaped at the tidings, every face shone with stern determination, every eye beamed with martial fire. They rushed on as if afraid they might arrive too late to get one shot at the slayers of their brethren. The Yankee blood is up at last. New England is in a blaze.

And now, when the morning gun is fired from the British lines in Boston, it is answered by a roar of defiance from Cambridge. The west wind brings across the broad bay the strange sound of drums beating the reveille in the Yankee camps. Battalions are taking post, and earthworks rising on Roxbury side. Bayonet for bayonet. Before General Gage realizes it, he and his ten thousand redcoats are shut up in Boston like rats in a trap. The rebels have turned the tables on him.

To destroy a few stores at Concord General Gage has brought on war. Why does he not march out at the head of his army, and disperse these rebels whose camp-fires blaze all around him?

The British generals Howe, Burgoyne, and Clinton, with reinforcements, have arrived. In order to pass away the time agreeably, the generals have brought their fishing-rods. Perhaps they may find more exciting sport waiting for them. At any rate the rebels will not let them go a fishing.

General Gage has made the townspeople give up their arms because he is afraid that if the rebels from the outside attack him, those inside the town will help them. He has promised to let all who will leave the town, but in a little time he has broken this promise.

However, many have gone, — many who have not a penny in the world to bless themselves with. It is enough to melt a heart of stone to see them straggling along the road over the Neck, with want before and starvation behind them. Even the king's officers are moved to pity as mothers, with their babes in their arms, or holding their little ones by the hand, and shedding tears, are thus driven from their once happy homes by the iron hand of war.

But sympathizing friends and a warm welcome await them. As fast as they come out they receive help to go to their friends in the country, and they are given this paper, which is a passport to the benevolent everywhere: —

"BOSTON, May 7, 1775.

"The Bearer Mrs. Mary Rose and her Family removing out of the town of Boston are recommended to the Charity and Assistance of our Benevolent Sympathizing Brethren in the several towns in this Province.

"By Order of the Committee of Donations.

"*Five in family.*   ALEX. HODGDON, *Clerk.*

"To the Selectmen and Committee of Correspondence in the several Towns in the Province of Massachusetts Bay."

Further to protect himself against the inhabitants, General Gage has built a small work on Beacon Hill, commanding the town.

He has all along had an eye to the heights of Dorchester and Charlestown, where he fears the rebels will erect batteries that can throw shot into the town. So far he has only pushed forward a battery of heavy guns on the Neck, opposite to Dorchester Heights, and the one we visited on Copp's Hill, opposite Charlestown. The frigate in the channel, between, cannot elevate her guns sufficiently to sweep these heights. So far, then, in spite of the knowledge of every drummer-boy in the army that whoever holds these hills is master of Boston, this is all that the British commander-in-chief has done. Perhaps he thinks the ships will keep the rebels at a distance. Perhaps, as he is so slow, the rebels will help him to act.

The Americans are not idle. By no means. They are improving the time in making raids on the harbor islands, burning the hay, carrying off the sheep, and doing whatever else may make the situation of the enemy in Boston more and more uncomfortable. So daring are the provincials become under the lead of Putnam and Warren that a British officer writes to his friend, "With you, who are so jealous of the honor of the British flag, I shall risk my credit if I tell you what insults have been offered to it with impunity; but indeed they are too many to relate."

Another says impatiently and bitterly, "The bravery

and daring are all on one side." "And to complete all,"
writes a third, "the admiral has had a boxing-match in
the streets, has got his eyes blackened, and his sword
broken by a gentleman of the town whom he had used
very ill and struck repeatedly before he returned his
blows."

Never were men more eager for a fight than those now
bearing the arms of King George, cooped up in Boston
town.

Well, there is going to be one, for the general has at
last determined to seize and fortify Dorchester Heights.
He is right. They are the key of Boston. Howe and
Clinton are to land with troops, march up the hills, and
erect the king's standard. They settle it that in the night
of the 18th of June this is to be done. That is easily
said.

But the secret has flown to the American camp. All of
General Gage's secrets do seem to have wings. Strong
reinforcements are poured into Roxbury. Detachments
of militia are hurried in. It really looks as if the first
important battle was to be on this side.

"We must have more elbow-room," said General Burgoyne significantly.

"Is it not about time we were doing something ourselves?" murmured the impatient young Americans at Cambridge.

So that on both sides there was the same eagerness to

be up and doing. This time it is the Americans who strike the first.

In the American Committee of Safety some one proposes to take possession of Bunker Hill and to fortify it; and the proposal, after due deliberation, is unanimously agreed to. The next step is to refer it to the general of the army and his council for execution. General Ward immediately calls his general officers together. In that group of men are Putnam and Thomas, Warren and Pomeroy, Spencer and Greene, Whitcomb and Heath, and perhaps the veteran Stark, who, although only a colonel, commands the New Hampshire troops.

These men sit around a table in the old Hastings House, near the College Green. They are to settle the plan and to fix the details. They have plenty of men, but little powder at command. It is first agreed that a thousand men shall be sent to throw up the intrenchments. Then the question comes up, How many cartridges shall be served out to each man?

For powder, we repeat, is so scarce that it is a question whether there is enough for battle.

"Sixty," said some of the younger men who had learned war from books, that being the number usually given to soldiers going into action.

"Five," said one veteran officer. "Let our men take aim as I do when I am hunting deer, and five rounds will be enough. Ten will certainly be more than enough."

These grizzled Indian hunters did not consider that shooting men and shooting deer were not quite the same thing to inexperienced soldiers. It was decided that fifteen rounds were enough.

It was also decided that the thousand men should be in part taken from Massachusetts, and in part from Connecticut regiments. Of course the honor of engaging in this battle belonged equally to all the officers and men of the army, whether they came from New Hampshire, Rhode Island, Connecticut, or the old Bay Colony. That is military law and usage too. Massachusetts called them to her aid. They were ready to lay down their lives in her cause; they submitted to be commanded by her officers for the good of this cause when it was necessary; but they would never have stirred from their camps had the right of their own officers equally to command been questioned. That would have been a downright insult, of which these Massachusetts men were incapable, to say, "When we order you must obey, but when you order we will do as we like." No; the army, such as it was, was one by the general consent of all the officers and soldiers in it, high or low, who understood quite well that without this subordination they were only an armed mob.

Thus this army of Cambridge and of Bunker Hill was the army of the New England Colonies, and not of Massachusetts alone; and wherever these soldiers served together, the officer highest in rank would be entitled to command.

The two men in this army most experienced in war are General Putnam of the Connecticut, and Colonel Stark of the New Hampshire, forces. Their fame and their presence are a tower of strength. The man in whom the army most relies, after these two, is General Warren, who is called general because he has just been elected one; but he has not yet received his commission of general. There are many other officers who have seen service, among them the brave Pomeroy, Frye, Prescott, and Nixon.

The thousand Massachusetts and Connecticut men, led on by Colonel Prescott, marched from Cambridge Common at nine in the evening of the 16th for Bunker Hill. Their intrenching tools were in carts. They had about three miles to go. When they came to the Neck General Putnam joined them, and put himself at their head.

This Neck is a strip of low and level land, washed on one side by the Charles and on the other by the Mystic. The Americans marched across unperceived.

Without noise, instead of taking the road through the town, they keep straight on up the slope of Bunker Hill. In a few minutes they reach the top and halt. This is the spot they are ordered to fortify.

But here a different decision is adopted. They take their arms again and continue on to Breed's Hill, at the farther end of the peninsula. And here, about midnight, they go to work like beavers, turning up the sod in the form of a square. All is quiet across the river, while

HEIGHTS OF CHARLESTOWN FROM THE NAVY YARD, 1826.

these men toil as if their lives depended on their efforts.
General Gage is waiting for the eighteenth day of the
month, and the seventeenth has not yet dawned.

The town continues buried in peaceful slumber, the
hill-top continues the scene of unceasing activity until
dawn. Then the scene changes.

Four in the morning. Daylight steals up the heavens.
Bang! goes a gun from the vessel in the ferry-way. It is
a shotted gun. Flash succeeds flash. Boom! boom!
answer the war-ships and floating batteries in the stream.
Louder and louder still swells the angry roar as the battery
on Copp's Hill, joining in, sends its shot bounding over
the crest of Breed's Hill among the workmen, cutting
long furrows in the grass, burying themselves in the
earth, sending tall jets of dust in the air, as they plunge
into the earthen walls. Each shot seems angrily seeking a
life. The young soldiers, on whom this iron hail is so
pitilessly falling, grow pale and nervous. They slacken
their efforts. It is a fearful ordeal for them. But Prescott mounts the walls, and walks slowly around the
parapet, coolly giving his orders. This contempt of danger
gives new courage. Cheer upon cheer rings out. Again
the men ply the spade with redoubled energy, and
momentarily the walls rise higher and higher.

At four in the morning this tremendous fire began. At
this early hour the crash of artillery, breaking the stillness,
and shaking the solid earth, turned the town of Boston

from its usual quiet into the wildest commotion. The
people rush into the streets, the soldiers to arms. Hark
to the drums! There go the trumpets! Consternation is
in every face, hurry and confusion is on every side,
while the artillery thunders unceasingly. Mounted officers dash through the streets; the barracks and camps
are alive with men hurrying on their equipments. There
is not much exultation here, but the bewilderment of surprise. The officers go upon the housetops, and, looking
across the river, see the American fortress looming black
and defiant and silent. What! will those poltroons of
Yankees stand that terrific cannonade? Will they not
scamper away in terror? No, they work on. Not a shot
answers the hurricane of iron hurled at them. They are
getting used to it.

"It is going to be a hot day," these Britons say under
their breath. They give one longing look out over the
blue waters of the bay to where the sea lies so tranquil.
Ah! England is over there, home is there. They go to
their chambers, and hurriedly write a few lines, — their
last will and testament. Such is a soldier's life.

General Gage calls his high officers around him in the
Province House. They have all seen the Yankee works.
All understand what they mean. It is a challenge.
Either come out and fight or submit to be driven from
Boston, are its terms.

Every general agrees that the Americans must be driven

from those heights, cost what it may. So the order is given to get twenty-five hundred of the best troops under arms. That will surely be more than enough. General Howe is ordered to lead them, with General Pigot as second in command. So certain are they that these raw Americans will run away when they see the compact columns of veterans bearing down upon them that the advice of one sagacious officer is neglected or overruled.

His advice is to land these troops at Charlestown Neck. One look convinces us that this plan would be fatal to the Americans. With twenty-five hundred men, supported by artillery, between them and retreat — behind the works they have erected — it is doubtful if a single man could escape. But this counsel is not followed. It is feared that this plan may expose General Gage's troops to an attack in front and rear at once, — in front from the provincials on Breed's Hill, in the rear from those at Cambridge. And thus timidity or infatuation, or both, rules the council of war.

His orders given and his troops embarked, General Gage ascends the steeple of the Old North, which commands the battle-field. Some one asks him if the rebels will stand. "Yes," he replies, "if one John Stark is there; for he is a brave fellow."

BUNKER HILL MONUMENT.

XIII.

THE SWORD OF BUNKER HILL.

FROM the heights of Breed's Hill every movement in the streets of Boston is plainly seen, — the artillerymen lashing their horses into a gallop, the solid bodies of infantry marching to the wharves. Soon a fleet of boats pushes out into the harbor, forming a long and glittering line protected by the guns of the shipping. Sweeping majestically on, this line is directed towards the extreme seaward point of Charlestown, Morton's Point.

Two in the afternoon, — a sultry day. The boats ground on the beach. The men, jumping on shore, quickly take their ranks. Then each regiment moves up the little hill[1] in front to its allotted place, until the battalions stand in three lines facing the rebel works. Let us look behind those works.

The redoubt, crowning the summit of Breed's Hill, is manned by a hundred and fifty or a hundred and sixty of the men who have built it. In the midst, calm as a summer's morn, stands Prescott. A bank of fresh earth, joining the redoubt, continues its face down the slope of the hill, towards the Mystic, about one hundred yards. This is well manned, but there is still a wide space open between it and the river, — wide enough for General Howe to march his whole army in columns of battalions straight through. The Americans have not half fortified their front.[2]

On the right of the redoubt fences and trees give protection to more men, then comes the steep hillside, at the foot of which is the town; and in the houses here a number of American marksmen have taken post. In a word,

[1] This hill was partly within the Navy Yard. See p. 165.
[2] Until the Connecticut and New Hampshire forces closed up this line absolutely nothing prevented the British from flanking the works on Breed's Hill. Bunker Hill was the post the Americans were ordered to take. It was more easily defended.

the redoubt and its defences cover only a part of the line along which, it is plain, the British mean to advance. Prescott will hold Breed's Hill if the enemy do not flank, or get behind him, but he cannot stop them.

Yet they must be stopped. This long gap must be filled.

There is a gray-headed soldier on the field who has the fire and energy of fifty men. He has experience. He is beloved and trusted as no other man there is. He sees that the battle will go against them if this fatal gap is not closed up. He has no aids, no orderlies, no guards, but if a thing is to be done he rides to the spot and gives his orders. And his orders are obeyed. That man is "Old Put." He is like an old war-horse who scents battle from afar, every sense quickened by the crisis. Now he is at this spot, now that. His foaming charger's side is bloody with spurring, his own face bathed in sweat; but these appearances are not caused by frenzy or excitement. Far from it. They are decision followed by action. The men who have never heard a shot fired in anger, who see two thousand of the flower of English soldiery ready at a word to rush upon them, and are shaken by the sight, look around them for a leader. And in this stern-visaged old man they behold him. But his bravery is so reckless that they expect to see him shot from his horse every moment.

Two hundred men with cannon are seen marching from the redoubt to the rear. Putnam spurs up to them.

"Draw up your men here," he commands, waving his sword towards a stone wall. The men catch fire, and with new spirit take the designated position. They pull up the fences and gather up armfuls of hay lying ready-mowed upon the field. With these rails and this grass they heap up a breastwork. It will not stop a bullet, but it gives them confidence. It is not a real, but a sham defence.

"Protect their legs, and your raw soldiers won't mind their heads," is one of "Old Put's" maxims.

Now the head of a column is seen mounting the slope of Bunker Hill. It is Stark's New Hampshire battalion, with their colonel intrepidly leading them through their first baptism of fire. They halt on the brow. Putnam rides up.

"Push on, Colonel Stark!" he says. "The enemy have landed and formed."

Stark's drums beat, and the gallant fellows marching steadily on to the hay breastwork, in their turn carry it along the front of the enemy quite to the river. The gap is closed up. It is now a hedge of steel behind which a thousand brave hearts beat high with the hope of victory. These men then sit down on the grass, and, having taken off their coats, proceed to pare the bullets served out to them with their jackknives, for hardly two muskets are of the same calibre.

Other troops come on the field, and join those at the hay

breastwork. It is some distance behind the redoubt, but
that is no matter. It is only straw, but the British
infantry cannot pass here except over the bodies of its
brave defenders. Stark is here with the keen-eyed
hunters of the White Hills. Reed is here with his New
Hampshire boys. The lion-hearted Knowlton is here.
And Putnam, who has brought up two more guns, and
pointed them with his own hand, is here.

Stark is as cool as ice and as hard as iron. Even the
smell of powder does not excite him. Walking deliberately out in front of his regiment, he plants a mark in
the ground. Then he as deliberately returns.

"When the enemy are there," he says, jerking his sword
toward the spot, "give it to them; but not before."

Putnam rides along the line, speaking to and en-
couraging the men. He tells them to lie down out of
reach of the enemy's balls until they are within good gunshot, but is heedless of his own person.

A group of officers is seen in consultation. Putnam
dismounts, loads one of the cannon with grape, points, and
discharges it with fatal effect. He then resumes his tour
of the lines; for right before him the enemy is massing
in columns of attack with the precision of a parade. The
decisive moment is at hand.

Who shall describe the excitement of this moment?
Crouched or kneeling behind their unfinished ramparts,
the farmers of New England confront the disciplined vet-

erans of Old England. At their head stand doctors, or lawyers, or other farmers like themselves, — soldiers in name, — every man fighting with a halter around his neck. For the fiftieth time they take aim, try the locks, or glance uneasily over their shoulders. Some put bullets between their teeth. Some offer up a silent prayer to God.

The veteran officers alone are cool.

"Wait for the word; don't fire till you can see the white of their eyes," is the order Putnam gives.

PROVINCIAL
CARTRIDGE-BOX.

The space between this unconquerable phalanx of New Hampshire and Connecticut soldiers is filled, or partly filled, by fragments of incomplete battalions of Massachusetts that have hurried to the field. And here the noble Warren, scorning the shelter of the redoubt, takes his stand, armed, like the common soldier, only with a musket. But he has already used that musket at Lexington and at Chelsea. Warren's presence and his example are worth a host.

For before the reinforcements came on, our poor fellows, daunted by the cannonade, and worn out with toil, believed they were abandoned to their fate. But now the bravest and truest stand along that embattled line from left to right, — Stark, Putnam, Pomeroy, Warren, Prescott. Not

Massachusetts alone, but Connecticut, New Hampshire, and Massachusetts, will fight this battle shoulder to shoulder, and to the death. Not to one colony alone will history record the deeds of this day, but to united New England, made one by a common cause. Eternal infamy reward the man who would wrest one jot or tittle of the fame justly due to all these heroes in order to bestow it on some favorite!

Warren and Putnam meet on the battle-field. "I am sorry to see you here, General Warren. Will you give me your orders?" asks the old hero.

"No," replies the chivalric young man. "But tell me where I can do the most good."

Pointing to the redoubt, Putnam says, "You will be covered there." He cannot see the hope and pride of the army fall a sacrifice to his burning zeal to distinguish himself.

"Don't think I came to seek a place of safety," replies the young soldier, "but tell me where the onset will be most furious."

Putnam still points to the redoubt, and thither Warren bends his steps. The soldiers welcome him with huzzas. Prescott hastens to meet him. "Will you take my command, General?" he asks.

"No," Warren replies, "the command is yours."

But he will not stay behind these walls. He sees the line between the breastwork and the hay-fence is most exposed, and here he takes his stand. He has at last found what he is seeking, — the post of honor and of danger. Noble refusal! heroic resolve! Let posterity applaud the one and history record the other.

The lines are formed. Thanks to Putnam, there is no weak spot now. At the redoubt the word is passed, "Don't waste a kernel of powder. Aim at the waistband; pick out the handsome coats." And so, from left to right, the provincials calmly await the attack.

General Howe pushes his artillery to the front. The cannoneers are at their pieces, with lighted matches. He has his proud battalions massed and ready to launch upon the despised peasants. All is ready. Still he hesitates. The rebel works look strong. They are full of men. He sends for reinforcements. General Gage promptly embarks two more battalions, which land nearer the town, under a galling fire from the Americans, posted in the houses. Seeing this, General Howe despatches a messenger to General Burgoyne, who is on Copp's Hill, with a request to throw some shells among these houses. The guns quickly open upon the town, and in a few minutes it is set on fire, its defenders retreating before the flames. The inhabitants are flying in terror from their homes.

Earl Percy is now furiously cannonading Roxbury from the Neck, Burgoyne Charlestown from Copp's Hill. All the church-steeples, all the housetops, of Boston are black with anxious spectators. Crowds throng the heights of

Malden and Chelsea. The air, thick with smoke, and trembling with explosions, hangs a dusky pall over land and sea. The battle begins.

Right and left the charging columns advance steadily toward the intrenchments, the artillery firing round after round at short range. Now the British are stopped by fences which throw them into disorder, increased by a brisk cannonade from the rail-fence. Putnam points these pieces, which make long lanes in the enemy's ranks. But the disciplined soldiers of the empire, closing up these gaps, march steadily onward.

General Howe leads the right attack in person. The picked soldiers of the whole army, grenadiers and light-infantry, move forward, a solid and imposing torrent of bayonets, at his command. Now they are within musket-range. Now the front ranks pour a rattling volley into the intrenchments. The British artillery ceases firing. Brown Bess and the bayonet must now decide the day.

As yet an ominous silence reigns behind that long mound of stones and hay, fringed with steel. Nearer, and nearer still, come the exulting and confident foe. What! will the "cowards," the "wretches," not fire one shot for the honor of New England — just one?

At last the foremost ranks touch the dead-line. For one instant the combatants see each other's eyes. Then the intrenchment blazes like a volcano. The hill trembles beneath the discharges, while its defenders are swallowed up in smoke and flame rolling down upon and engulfing their assailants. And in this murky cloud, lighted by incessant flashes, death is reaping a rich harvest.

As the smoke slowly rises, the dead lie in heaps. For them drum or trumpet shall no more sound the charge. Awful is the carnage. The whole head of the assaulting column is destroyed. For an instant or two it wavers, then recoils, then turns, and pours a tide of fugitives down the hill. Well done the rail-fence!

The officers, stung by the disgrace, vainly endeavor to stem this tide. But it is useless. They, too, are borne along with it. And as they are thrust aside by their panic-struck men, something wounds them still more. It is the cheers of the victors, mingled with shouts of, "Say, are the Yankees cowards now?"

While the combat at the rail-fence is proceeding, an equal force of the enemy, under General Pigot, furiously assails the redoubt and breastwork. It is allowed to come within thirty yards. Then a close and murderous fire begins. Few of the assaulting column reach the ditch alive. The same fatal accuracy distinguishes the American fire; the same butchery is going on all along the whole line. Pigot cannot advance. It is a complete, an awful repulse.

General Gage witnesses this catastrophe from the steeple. Not a moment must be lost. He hurries to Howe's assistance all the remaining troops at his disposal.

So far the American loss is trifling. The enemy fire too high, and their balls, cutting the limbs of the trees which cover our men, strew the ground with the litter.

While the British general is making superhuman exertions to rally his men for a second assault, there is a short respite.

BOSTON FROM BREED'S HILL, 1791.

Putnam, again mounting his horse, dashes back over the ridge to Bunker Hill, where there are hundreds of men whose officers cannot or will not lead them to the front. He entreats, he commands them by turns. He sees an artillery officer taking his guns off the field, and, riding up, peremptorily orders him back to his post. The officer refuses. Then Putnam tells him if he does not obey he will cut him down on the spot. Sullenly the officer obeys. Then to the Neck, where there are crowds, perplexed by contradictory orders or too cowardly to face the hot fire through which the general has just come as if he bore a charmed life. Only a few straggling bodies reward these exertions of the commander by marching to the lines. Still is he the ruling spirit of the hour, still he leaves nothing untried or undone; and as he cannot coax or drive the recreants to their duty, his place is with those who are again preparing to meet a second and still more desperate onset.

For now the British general, gathering his broken and dispirited battalions together, again leads them on to the assault. They meet with a second, and if possible more appalling disaster than before. This time the men throw their arms away, and, rushing to the waterside, fling themselves into the boats. It is a veritable panic. The crews drive them out with curses and with blows, like dogs. Their own captains beat and prick them with their sabres. But at last discipline prevails; at last they are huddled together in some order, and, seeing their reinforcements land on the beach, close under the redoubt, take courage, and once more re-form their decimated ranks. Although enemies, we cannot refuse this heroic courage our admiration.

On their side the Americans load and fire with amazing rapidity and accuracy. The enemy's officers advance to the front only to be picked off. "There! see that officer!" is the signal for a fatal volley. General Howe finds himself standing alone. All his aids have been disabled. His faithful servant brings him a bottle of wine, which is dashed from his hand before he can drink. At this moment a single disciplined battalion could have captured or driven the whole of them into the sea.

All this General Gage sees. It is defeat, it is dishonor. To him it is ruin. General Clinton sees it. An heroic impulse prompts him. He throws himself into a boat, crosses the river, and puts himself at the head of the fresh troops. A hurried consultation takes place. The rail-fence cannot be taken. Howe will not risk a third attempt. Half his fine army is already destroyed. It is decided to attack the redoubt on all sides simultaneously with the bayonet.

The order is given, and for the third time the attacking columns are hurled against the redoubt. The provincials have exhausted their ammunition, but think not of retreat. On both sides is the courage of desperation.

The weary defenders of the redoubt, overcome by their previous efforts, have imbibed the spirit of their indomitable leader. Not a man stirs. Awaiting the advance of the scarlet line, with grim determination they hold their fire until the enemy are close to the trenches. It is shockingly fatal. Again the enemy is staggered, but the American fire is now no longer the terrific fusillade of the first and second attacks. The enemy press on. On their left the Marines and the 47th, rallying from the confusion caused by the first volley, leap the ditch and climb the parapet under a sore and heavy fire. Two captains fall in gaining it. Three captains of the 52d are killed on the parapet. Captain Harris of the 5th, who has distinguished himself at Lexington, is shot down in the act of mounting it. For a few moments the resistance is as stubborn as the onset is furious, but the Americans are now no longer able to maintain the combat upon equal terms. Their powder is gone. The royal troops crowd the parapet, from which they fire down into the faces of the provincials. An officer of noble bearing haughtily demands the surrender of the garrison, but falls dead almost as soon as the words are uttered. Furious, raging, like a lion at bay, Prescott's voice rises above the horrible din. The Americans fight like madmen. They wrench the muskets from the hands of their assailants, and with them bayonet their owners. Some hurl stones, and others club their now useless weapons in sheer desperation. A horrible and sanguinary *melée* rages within the four walls of the redoubt, above which rise clouds of dust that blind the combatants. Twice does Prescott's little band clear the redoubt of enemies, but the exasperated Britons return to the charge with a determination to conquer or die. Step by step, they make a road with the bayonet, forcing the defenders backwards toward the gorge. While this unheard-of resistance is going on, sharp musketry begins in the rear of the redoubt. The cry arises that the Americans are surrounded. Prescott now tells his men to save themselves. Crowded with dead and dying, the bloodstained fortress is at last in possession of the triumphant enemy.

With the fall of the redoubt the breastwork is deserted, and the enemy begins to show in force in the rear of this part of the line. Warren's men, who have securely held the gap against the renewed efforts of the grenadiers, are now between two fires, and are, in their turn, compelled to beat a hasty retreat. While doing so a ball strikes down their brave leader, who meets a soldier's death.

RELICS FROM WARREN'S BODY.

The redoubt and its defences are in the enemy's hands. They use the bayonet with cruel effect. Prescott and his men are in disorderly retreat. A rout is imminent. The day is lost. But now, as their right flank is uncovered, the provincials, who have firmly held the rail-fence, still presenting an undaunted front, fall back fighting to Bunker Hill, from which a few brave men advance to aid their comrades. The rout is thus checked, the enemy kept at bay, and time given for the fugitives to make good their retreat across the Neck, under the heavy fire of the enemy's floating batteries, which sweep it with continued discharges of grape and round shot.

On Bunker Hill a last heroic effort is making to rally the Americans. The commanding voice of Putnam rises above the confusion beseeching the stragglers "In God's name to form and give them one shot more!" But neither he, nor those other brave spirits who rally around him, can stem the tide. Here, too, men are falling fast. At last Bunker Hill is abandoned to the enemy, who plants his artillery on its brow, and opens upon the retreating Americans a plunging fire.

With those true hearts whom he can still hold together, Putnam retreats no farther than the first defensible position, — Prospect Hill. Here he again faces the enemy. In this act we recognize the leader. First in the field, and last to leave it, "Old Put" throws himself boldly in the path of the victorious foe.

There is no exultation in the ranks of the enemy. They have carried one little hill at the cost of more than a thousand men. A victory! They do not inscribe "Bunker Hill" on their standards. A victory! They are aghast at the price they have paid for the lesson that "Yankees will fight." They have, indeed, saved Boston for the moment; they have saved their honor. And yet have they received such a stunning blow that "Bunker Hill," traced in letters of blood, shall stand on the page of history as a field of humiliation, not for England's arms, but for English arrogance and presumption.

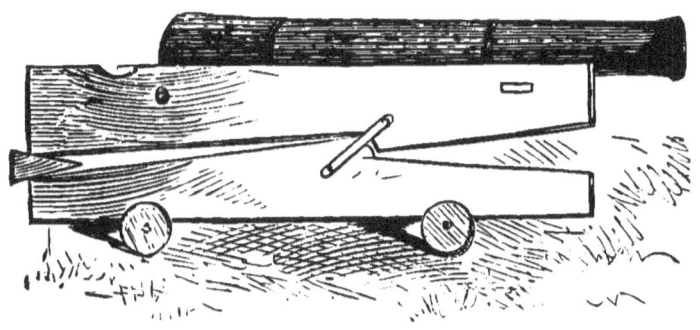

AMERICAN SIEGE GUN AND CARRIAGE.

XIV.

YANKEE DOODLE.

A FINE despatch General Gage will have to send home to his king. It will be something in these terms: —

"Please your Majesty the army of subjugation has had a battle forced upon it, in which it has lost more than two to the enemy's one, with many valuable officers slain. Behaving with their ancient valor, your Majesty's veteran troops drove the raw levies of the rebels from all their positions at the point of the bayonet. We have won a glorious victory.

"P. S. — Your Majesty's army remains cooped up in Boston. The rebels are burrowing, like rabbits, all around us. But 't was a splendid victory!"

One officer, who does not pick and choose his words in order to gloss over a sad disaster, writes home: —

"You good people of Old England will find out that some other mode must be adopted than gaining every little hill at the expense of a thousand Englishmen."

And, on the other side of the lines, our brave General Greene, of Rhode Island, writes to his friends: —

"I wish we could sell them another hill at the same price."

The Americans, not knowing how they have crippled him, believe the enemy's next move will be on Cambridge. General Putnam is therefore making superhuman exertions at Prospect Hill to stop him.

The British, feeling far from secure with such a numerous and audacious foe before them, are only intent upon protecting themselves from attack by strongly intrenching on Bunker Hill. For the present, spades are trumps.

Here we commence our tour of the American works. We find, first, —

Our pickets continuing to annoy the enemy from the deserted houses beyond Charlestown Neck, until driven out by his cannon. These houses are then burned to the ground; but the ruins still afford a shelter to our marksmen, who fire whenever they can get a shot at the British fatigue-parties. To stop this, two armed gondolas, with raised bulwarks, are brought up the Mystic River, and fire on our men at intervals. Thus, the Americans, though beaten on the 17th, have not ceased to hold an advanced post within musket-shot of the enemy. And from this post they will not be dislodged.

Nature has placed some formidable obstacles in the way of an enemy marching on Cambridge in this direction. A group of hills occupies all the ground between the Mystic River and Cambridge marshes. Among these, lifted high above the others, is Prospect Hill. Well is it named, for it commands all the region surrounding. The high-road from Charlestown to Cambridge passes directly underneath it. It is about equally distant from our advanced post at the Neck and the main army at Cambridge. Every movement of the enemy on Bunker Hill can be seen from its summit, as well as every demonstration by his ships of war; for having sole command of the water, his armed vessels may easily move up the Mystic on one side and bombard the New Hampshire troops at Medford, or they may work up the Charles on the other, and shell the camps at Cambridge.

To go back a little. On the evening of the glorious 19th of April, when the dispirited soldiers of the king retreated in disorder over Charlestown Neck by this road, our own victorious yeomanry pursued them nearly to the foot of Bunker Hill. It was just at this critical moment, while Lord Percy's men were hurrying on around the foot of Prospect Hill, that seven hundred American militia, who had not yet fired a shot, were marching over this hill from Medford. A few minutes earlier would have brought them upon the British flank. But they were too late.

Seeing the British safe on Bunker Hill, and it being now too dark to distinguish friend from foe, our men fell back as far as Prospect Hill, first posting sentinels at the Neck. After the necessary pickets were placed at various points on the road, the main body moved back to Cambridge. Here, at the foot of Prospect Hill, was mounted the first guard of the Revolution, April 19, 1775.

Stark's camp, on Winter Hill, and Putnam's own around Inman's farm,[1] are each about half a mile distant from the new position Putnam has selected, which he has been fortifying since the afternoon of the 17th. Stark is also throwing up works to cover his own encampment. Thus we see that Putnam may either call Stark, or the troops at Inman's, to his aid, or march to the help of either, as necessity may demand, long before the enemy can strike a blow; and he has the whole army at his back in case of need.

Prospect Hill is, therefore, the key to the American position so long as the army remains on the defensive, as it now must. Keenly alive to its importance, knowing that moments are now precious, scorning fatigue as well as danger, it is our gallant Putnam who is making incredible efforts to put this hill in a thorough state of defence.

---

[1] Inman's house stood on what is now Inman Street, Cambridge.

Throughout Saturday night and far into Sunday, mattock and spade are unceasingly plied. Here Putnam's son finds his father among the workmen, giving his orders, never having taken off his clothes since the day before the battle.

The greatest want on our side is not men, but artillery, with which to defend these works. All the old iron cannon that can be found far or near have been carefully collected, but many are condemned pieces, and threaten greater injury to their owners than to the enemy; many are honeycombed with age, or have had their trunnions knocked off to render them useless. Yankee ingenuity will, however, remedy this last defect. The guns are ingeniously bedded in timber carriages, in the same way as a musket-barrel in a stock. But it takes a long time to elevate or depress these unwieldy machines. Powder, too, is scarce, and must be saved for battle, and not wasted at long bowls. The enemy pitch shot and shell into our lines, but our soldiers are getting used to "ducking" when the sentinels cry out "A shot!"

As for the camps, they are a curious medley indeed. Some of the huts are made of boards, some of sail-cloth; some partly of one and partly of the other. Others are built of stones and sods, bricks and brush. Others, again, are ingeniously contrived of wicker-work, and look like bee-hives. Now and then some lucky officer has a tent; but none of the troops have come regularly equipped for the field except the Rhode Islanders, who have tents, and whose camp is laid out in exact military order.

Leaving Prospect Hill, and descending into the road again, we find earthworks thrown up to command the cross-road leading to Lechmere's Point.[1] These too are well manned. This is Patterson's post. The Americans have an eye to this approach, because the enemy landed at the Point and marched this way to Concord. That is why a force has been concentrated at Inman's with an advanced post here.

HESSIAN FLAG.[2]

We now understand that before the battle of Bunker Hill the Connecticut troops under Putnam, and the New Hampshire levies under Stark, covered the left of the army at Cambridge, and would have received the enemy's first blows.

---

[1] These works were at, or near, what is now Union Square, Somerville.

[2] Two years later, in 1777, the army of General Burgoyne was quartered on these hills, — the British on Prospect Hill, the Hessians on Winter Hill. They were taken, bag and baggage, at Saratoga.

Having now passed the outworks, we keep along the highway until within five eighths of a mile from Cambridge Common, when we come upon more works on each side of the road, where it crosses a small stream.[1] Butler's Hill,[2] the eminence rising now on our left, is also being strongly intrenched on its brow and slopes. These works defend the camps at Cambridge, and will, when finished, close up the line from Charlestown road to Charles River.

Passing the sentinels here, a few minutes' walk brings us within sight of the college buildings. On both sides of us the fields and pastures are occupied by bodies of armed men engaged in cooking, drilling, or cleaning their arms. A few steps more and we enter the bustle and stir incident to the presence of a large force. We inquire of the first soldier we meet the way to headquarters, and he points out a gambrel-roofed house overlooking the Common. We halt here.

[1] Near the intersection of Beacon Street. The stream, now dry, was a branch of Miller's River.
[2] Dana Hill.

XV.

THE NEW ENGLAND ARMY.[1]

OLD MILE-STONE.

BEFORE it became a camp Cambridge was, and has continued from time to time to be, the seat of the insurrectionary government. The authority of the royal governor and council is of course denied, and has ceased outside of Boston. The old House of Representatives, no longer permitted to assemble, has given place to a Provincial Congress, whose orders are carried out by a select body called a Committee of Safety. In this way the government of the people, such as it is, goes on; but they have no courts of justice, nor can they have the stability and order of peaceful times in such a crisis as the present.

---

[1] This is the name given to it by the supreme authority of Massachusetts, in its official account of the Battle of Bunker Hill.

Notwithstanding hostilities have actually begun, the representatives of the people, or a majority of them, still cling to their king like a Hindoo to his idol. For them the throne is invested with a certain sacredness, which we call divine right. They have been so long used to calling themselves "subjects," and to going down upon their knees, that the idea of being free men is doubtfully balanced as a boon or an evil. And even now, when the cannon of Bunker Hill have scarcely ceased thundering the knell of this delusion in their ears, they cannot believe that their king will not right them at last. And he the most obstinate and vindictive man in all his broad kingdom! So they continue praying for King George, while shooting his soldiers, as it were, under protest.

But they do not know their man. His thick German blood is up. His rebellious subjects tender their petitions with one hand, while the other holds the sword. They do not offer the hilt in token of submission, but the point. In a way, they solicit his royal clemency while putting a pistol to his ear. So the king is now in a right royal fit of exasperation. He determines and on his royal word says accordingly these audacious colonists must be "chastised." He sputters and fumes. His ministers run to and fro. His arsenals and dockyards redouble their activity. His generals tell him America is as good as conquered. But this is not enough to satisfy George, "by the grace of God, king, etc., etc." England, and Scotland,

and Ireland are not enough to grind his traitorous subjects to powder. Gold has no smell: he will buy soldiers at so much a head. He writes to his continental neighbors for help. Proud old England shakes her purse in the faces of these beggarly princes. Hessians and Hanoverians are hired to fight Americans, with whom they have not even the shadow of a quarrel. Truly, a most noble and royal alliance for England! But the Empress Catharine — honor to her for the act! — refuses to sell her legions to do this dirty work. The king wrote to her with his own hand, but instead of replying in the same manner the great empress told her minister to answer this little king. She snubs him. She lets him know he does not understand his business of king.

These reflections and this retrospect have occupied the moments while our eyes ran over the scenes around us; and they naturally came to answer the mute inquiry of "What do all these formidable preparations mean?" "How will it all end?"

By the number of horses saddled and hitched to the trees, or the palings, as well as by the number of people going in or coming out, we should be able to identify the army headquarters. There is a sentinel at the door, but among the visitors a certain republican simplicity and equality is apparent, very different from the formality and etiquette surrounding the Province House. The post-rider's lank beast quietly crops the grass by the side of the general's sleek nag. And what insignia of rank officers may now and then have seem worn more with an eye to effect than fitness. It would be hard indeed, from any outward evidence, to tell which was the general and which the private soldier.

HOLDEN CHAPEL.

Only the shadow of discipline has entered this republican encampment, for soldiers accost their officers without hesitation and without troubling themselves to carry their hands to their cocked hats. In all those things which instil a sentiment of pride into an army our own is, we must admit, sadly deficient. No wonder the British laugh. Our soldiers can hardly help laughing at themselves.

It was in this house, however, that the battle of the 17th was planned. It was to this door couriers rode in hot haste during that bloody day. It is here that many of the young officers who thirst for renown have received their first commissions in the "Army of Liberty." Benedict Arnold, a young Connecticut soldier, is one of them. Here General Ward continues to direct the army as its commander-in-chief. Over that threshold pass Putnam, Thomas, Greene, Pomeroy, Stark, Heath, Spencer, Frye, and Whitcomb to consult, suggest, or pay simple visits of ceremony.

To the right, and in plain view, extends the Common, which is the parade-ground of the army. To the left, half hid among trees, rise the quaint roofs of the college halls, with the steeple of the meeting-house and the tower of the Episcopal Church beyond. Deserted by the professors, the tutors, and the students, the college buildings are now used as barracks and for the various offices connected with the administration of the army.

So the house of the college-steward, Jonathan Hastings, has the honor of being the headquarters, while in yonder academic halls young soldiers now learn the art of war instead of Greek and Latin.

First in order, and fronting the road, is Holden Chapel. Next to this, and farther back, is Hollis. We then come to three buildings forming three sides of a square. Haryard, named for the founder of the college, is the first, Stoughton, at the bottom of the square, is the second, and Massachusetts the third. The ground enclosed by these three structures is the college-yard, which in the old days

HARVARD HALL.

has witnessed many curious things, not the least being the burning of books written to prove witchcraft a humbug. In those days, too, for grave offences students were publicly whipped.

Of these three buildings, Harvard is the newest, Stoughton the oldest. The old Harvard Hall built in 1674, the most ancient structure, was burned a dozen years ago, and with it the college library and philosophical apparatus with "two compleat skeletons." It was, however, speedily rebuilt.[1]

We recollect that the first printing-press in North America was set up in the Indian College, a brick building of two stories, erected by the Society for Propagating

MASSACHUSETTS HALL.

the Gospel. Here were printed the Bay Psalm Book, and Eliot's Indian Bible, that wonderful monument of human perseverance and human skill. But now we find in Stoughton a printing-office having the official sanction of

[1] Of the ancient buildings now standing, Massachusetts, built in 1720, is the oldest. The old Stoughton, built in 1698, being very ruinous, was pulled down and rebuilt early in the present century on its present site.

the Province, issuing the "New England Chronicle and Essex Gazette" newspaper, which is eagerly read by the soldiers. Patriotic songs and ballads worked off on this press, and hawked about the camps, keep alive the martial spirit and enliven the hours of relaxation from duty. Here is a verse or two of one of the most popular: —

"Look on our Wives and Infants, they pit'ously implore
To be preserved from Blood Hounds who now invest our Shore.
O! let not those helpless Innocents become the lawless Prey
Of Dogs, of Dogs, of Dogs, of Dogs who hate America.

"Determin'd fix the bayonet and charge the sure Fusee,
Resolv'd like ancient Romans to set our Country Free,
And by the noble acts perform'd forever and for aye,
Prove that we are true Sons, true Sons of great America."

Nothing puts so much life in the soldier as a good song, well sung, inciting him to deeds of heroism. He goes into battle singing his national hymn with a cheerfulness and courage nothing else will arouse. The old French proverb, "They sing, they will pay," might aptly be changed into "They sing, they will fight." If soldiers are ready to drop with fatigue, let some one but strike up a spirited song, and the heavy feet fall once more together, the straggling files close up, while a thousand throats swell the chorus. An army without its war-songs will always be beaten by an army which sings.

From the college buildings, a few steps brings us to the meeting-house in which the first Provincial Congress assembled. Here was made the organization of the minute-men. Here Preble, Ward, and Pomeroy received their appointments. And here was formed the important Com-

THE PRESIDENT'S HOUSE.

mittee of Safety.[1] Thus does the meeting-house still play its part as in the old Puritan days.

But in these troublous times not even the Sabbath can be strictly regarded. The Massachusetts Congress has held its sessions on this sacred day; but what discipline

[1] This edifice stood near Dane Hall.

could not do for the Sabbath in camp the religious education of all these men makes a day of perfect order and quiet. In all the camps the army chaplains have attentive listeners, who are told and believe that the God of Battles is on their side.

Our tour of the college, and our investigation of its relation to the formation of the grand army of liberty, naturally ends at the president's house, which is just entering its fiftieth year, and in which successive presidents of the college have lived and died. In the old burying-ground, on the other side of the Common, we may read some of the long and pompous Latin epitaphs to their memory; and among the graves we shall find, now and then, a leaden coat-of-arms missing, and a little pool of water in the place it once occupied. The soldiers have quietly dug the lead from the tombstones and run it into bullets.

Before leaving the president's house, we may perhaps have the curiosity to see the form under which students are admitted. Here it is.

"CHAP. I. Part of Law 2d.

"The parents or guardians of those who have been accepted on examination, or some other person for them, shall pay to the steward three pounds in advance, towards defraying their college charges; also shall give bond to the President and Fellows of Harvard College with one or more sureties, to the satisfaction of the steward, in the sum of two hundred ounces of silver, to pay college dues quarterly, as they shall be charged in their quarter bills, according to the Laws and Customs of the College," etc.

Upon receiving from the steward a certificate that he had complied with the above law, the student could obtain from the president the following order of admission: —

"CANTABRIGIAE, August

"Admittatur in Collegium Harvardinum, A. B.

"*Praeses.*"

XVI.

WASHINGTON.

THE colonies have resolved to make common cause. Their Congress, sitting at Philadelphia, has at length assumed the supreme direction of affairs. It declares them to be not a nation, indeed, but "The Twelve United Colonies." And this is something out of which a nation may come. It has definitely adopted the army at Cambridge, hitherto the army of New England, as its own. So far it has lifted off the fearful responsibility from her shoulders. It has made choice of one of its own number, a delegate from Virginia, to command this army. This news will not be so pleasing. When the ballots are counted, John Hancock, rising from the president's chair, says, in a few words: —

"Colonel Washington, the Congress has made choice of you to be Commander-in-chief. I congratulate you, sir, upon this high honor."

This man's modesty was such that we are told he rushed from the hall when his name was first mentioned in connection with the office.

Six feet tall, in the prime of life, a noble and commanding figure rose in the midst of the delegates. Accepting the high trust, Colonel Washington must have won all hearts by the modesty with which he declared himself unequal to it. Although he has never seen one pitched battle, nor commanded scarcely any other troops than forest rangers, into his hands are committed the destinies of the Revolution. For diplomacy can now do nothing; arms must decide.

The very day on which General Washington received his commission, the New England army was having its deadly struggle on Bunker Hill.

Congress has also appointed four major-generals. They are Artemas Ward, Charles Lee, Philip Schuyler, and Israel Putnam. An adjutant-general and eight brigadiers are also appointed. Gates, the adjutant-general, Lee, and Schuyler set out with Washington for the army. The general carries the other commissions with him, to be delivered in person.

At New York, the General, first hearing of the battle of Bunker Hill, eagerly inquires how the Americans behaved, and if they stood the British fire. These are the men he is going to lead. His anxiety is therefore quite natural.

The courier tells him they fought like brave men. "Then," exclaimed the General, his doubts set at rest, "the liberties of the country are safe."

On Sunday, escorted by a troop of horse, and a cavalcade of citizens, the General enters Cambridge, passes one by one the elegant Tory mansions that skirt the road to Watertown, and dismounts at the army headquarters, — Jonathan Hastings's house.[1] The thunder of the enemy's guns notifies him that he has at last arrived.

In this house he is cordially welcomed by General Ward and the superior officers of the army, who have assembled here, and who are anxious to see what their future commander is like. They see he is every inch a man, — his manner noble and dignified, yet kind and winning. There is doubtless much whispering and many running comments upon his personal appearance, which we cannot help associating with character, after all. Not all were pleased that a Virginian is sent to take precedence of New England men; but all see that he is one born to command, and that to-morrow the army will have a head.

So George Washington eats his first dinner in this house with his future brothers-in-arms. And they give him a hearty, old-fashioned, New England welcome, as they can

---

[1] It is related that once, when Washington was travelling in Connecticut on Sunday, he was stopped by a constable, who inquired of the coachman if there was any urgent reason for travelling on the Lord's Day. The General himself explained, with great civility, why he had found it necessary to continue his journey on that day, assuring the officer that nothing was further from his intention than to treat with disrespect the laws of Connecticut relative to the Sabbath.

do when they will. After dinner Adjutant Gibbs, of
Glover's regiment, is hoisted, chair and all, upon the

THE WASHINGTON ELM, CAMBRIDGE.

table, and sings a rollicking camp-song. In this way
the General meets the future commander of his bodyguard.

The enemy celebrates the arrival of the new rebel commander by pounding furiously away at Roxbury with shot
and shell.

On Monday, the third day of the month, Washington
takes command of the army. He puts on his blue and

buff uniform, buckles on his sword, and, surrounded by his staff-officers, rides to the Common. It is a momentous act. The noble elm, under which he reins his horse, spreads its canopy of green over his head, while the columns of the army defile before him. All those thousands of eyes are fixed upon a single man, who curbs his fiery war-horse with a wrist of iron while graciously lifting his chapeau as the officers drop the points of their swords. Drums roll, fifes scream, huzzas fill the air, while the ground quakes under the tramp of this host.

At sight of this figure, so godlike in his manhood, so calm and reliant in his bearing, in whose every gesture authority is felt, a thrill runs through the ranks. The halo of victory seems surrounding the warrior's head.

Half-armed, clothed in homespun; no flag, no traditions, no country to call its own, no discipline; floating in uncertainty, friendless among nations; no arsenals, no navy, no unity of purpose or of will,— this motley army marches by its new leader. He and they are rebels and traitors. If he fail, the halter awaits him. But should he win!

Well, the review is over. Washington canters off to his quarters. The regiments return to their barracks or camps.

This day begins a new order of things. The army is formed into three corps. Ward commands the right, at Roxbury; Putnam the centre, at Cambridge; and Lee the left, at Charlestown and Medford. Orders are read at the head of the regiments, discipline enforced, and officers made to know their duty and to do it.

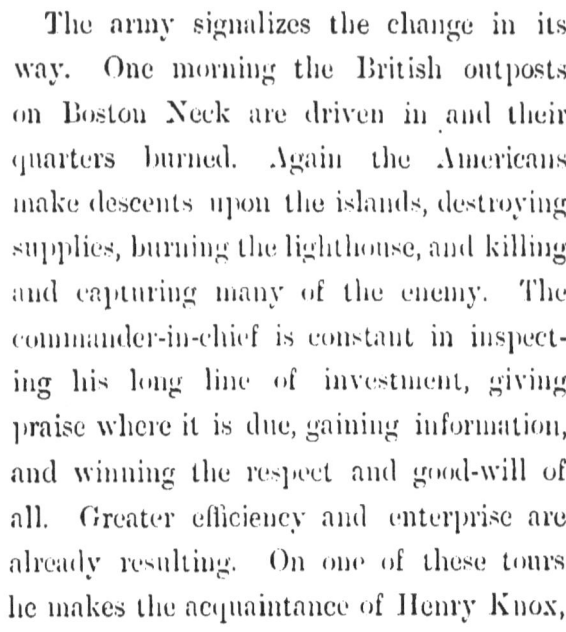

The army signalizes the change in its way. One morning the British outposts on Boston Neck are driven in and their quarters burned. Again the Americans make descents upon the islands, destroying supplies, burning the lighthouse, and killing and capturing many of the enemy. The commander-in-chief is constant in inspecting his long line of investment, giving praise where it is due, gaining information, and winning the respect and good-will of all. Greater efficiency and enterprise are already resulting. On one of these tours he makes the acquaintance of Henry Knox, the Boston bookseller, turned engineer.

EARLY AMERICAN FLAG.

The British are angry and vexed because it is almost always the Americans who attack. Besides, the rebel army has swept the country and islands so clean that it is difficult to get fresh meat to eat at any price. That same officer who not long ago wrote home that he and his comrades were living on the fat of the land, now tells this story : —

"If a boat, as sometimes happens, comes in with a few

half-starved sheep, we must pay a shilling a pound, or eat
no mutton."

And a civilian within the town confirms it thus dolefully : —

"We have now and then a carcass offered for sale in
the market, which formerly we would not have picked up
in the street. .... Was it not for a trifle of salt provisions that we have, 't would be impossible for us to live.
Pork and beans one day, and beans and pork another, and
fish when we can catch it."

The General has finally settled down in the fine old
Vassall House, on the Watertown road, which, being
deserted by its Tory owner, has been first occupied by
Glover's Marblehead regiment, composed of sailors, turned
soldiers, who handle the oar and the musket equally well.
It is a beautiful country-seat, this house, fronting the
meadows through which the crooked Charles winds in
glossy folds to the ocean. The hills of Little Cambridge
and of Brookline, across the river, show clumps of forest,
orchards, fields of yellow grain, with here and there a
steeple, or a country-house, gleaming in the sun. The landscape is delicious, it is so peaceful. Then the house
itself is airy and spacious. It was built by a gentleman
of birth and fortune, who little dreamed that he would
become an exile and his stately mansion be appropriated
to the uses of war. Its exterior is imposing, its interior
decorations and carvings tasteful, and even elegant. A

touch of the old refinement, which even a rude soldiery have not been able to drive away, lingers in the drawing-room, the wide entrance-hall, the wainscoted bed-chambers. The General is himself a man of aristocratic feelings. The house has a certain air of distinction. He is taken with it, and so henceforth and ever it is to be known as General Washington's headquarters.

But the ease, the luxury, the unbroken quiet, which once made Cambridge so inviting a residence, and this house a palace of indolence over which the hours stole unperceived, must now give place to action, frugality, and bustle. There is work to be done. All this multitude, called an army, must be made one in reality; while, at the same time, the enemy is watched, and checked, and menaced. The heart of the leader may have often sunk within him when he came face to face with his herculean task. But he keeps a bold and confident front. Such a man may die, but he is never vanquished.

First the army is thrown into brigades to give it form and mobility. Then Washington determines to make the defensive line between the Charles and Mystic so strong that it cannot be forced. Ploughed Hill,[1] then Cobble Hill,[2] and finally Lechmere's Point,[3] are covered with earthworks, trenches, and redoubts. The enemy does not know that there are no cannon for these batteries; he

[1] Since called Mt. Benedict. [2] Site of the McLean Asylum.
[3] East Cambridge.

WASHINGTON'S HEADQUARTERS.

does not know there is no powder for the cannon; he does not know that there are not men enough to man these long lines.

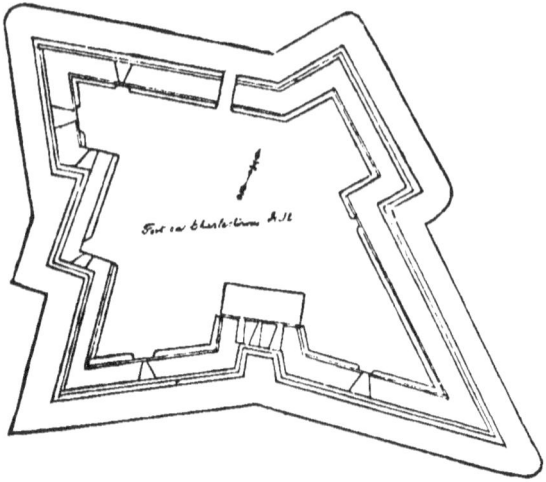

FORT ON COBBLE HILL.

General Gage, when he finds it necessary to communicate with his adversary by a flag of truce, addresses him as "George Washington, Esq." They sharpen their pens very much as they would their swords against each other, these men who had fought and campaigned together not many years ago.

Lively skirmishing goes on all the time between the outposts at Boston and Charlestown Neck. The Americans have been reinforced by a regiment of riflemen from Virginia and Pennsylvania, who have marched all the way to join the army.

These men have a dress — uniform it cannot be called — more savage than civilized, but still very serviceable and picturesque. It is a coarse brown linen hunting-shirt, or frock, with a cape, ornamented by a fringe, and secured at the waist by a belt, in which a knife and tomahawk are stuck. They also wear leggings and moccasins, like Indians, worked with beads and brilliantly dyed porcupine quills. They also march in Indian file. They fight like Indians, from whom they have really learned the art of war. They understand it to be their business to kill an enemy whenever they can draw a bead on him. And as soon as they arrived, Washington having sent them at once to the advanced posts, they began rifle practice at five hundred yards upon the British working and skirmishing parties.

FLAG OF MORGAN'S RIFLES.

But their dress is not so strange as their weapons, which until now have not been seen in the American camps. They carry a ball of small calibre, with accuracy, eight hundred yards. The British officers and men, while taking a quiet promenade or observation of our lines, outside their works, supposing themselves far out of range, are knocked over by a bullet not much larger than a buckshot. Presently one or two riflemen were captured, and their arms and dress examined with much curiosity. The Britons wrote to their friends at home accounts of these new enemies, whom they style " shirt-tail men, with their cursed twisted guns, — the most fatal widow-and-orphan makers in the world."

When these backwoodsmen first arrived in camp they were laughed at by their Northern comrades. This provoked angry words, then blows, between them and Glover's Marblehead men. A riot, which the officers found it impossible to quell, was the result. Glover threw himself on his horse and galloped post-haste to headquarters. He informed the General that his own and the Virginia regiment were in a state of mutiny. The General rose, and mounting his horse, which was always kept ready saddled, rode quickly to the spot, arriving at the moment when the uproar had reached its highest point. To get at the mutineers a field had to be crossed. While his black servant was in the act of letting down the bars the General, putting spurs to his horse, cleared them over Pompey's head, and dashed in among the rioters, who fell back to the right and left before him. Throwing his bridle to his servant, the General seized a tall, brawny rifleman by the throat with each hand, and began shaking and reproaching them at the same time. His great physical strength, now seen for the first time, his commanding presence, his energetic action, caused a moment's lull in the combat. Washington seized the advantage. He called the officers to him, and with their help the disgraceful affair was stopped. He then mounted his horse and rode back to his quarters, leaving officers and soldiers alike stupefied with what they had witnessed.

To besiege Boston cannon must be had, mortars, and munitions. Accordingly great is the rejoicing when it is known in camp that Captain Manly with his privateer, Lee, has captured and taken into Marblehead a British brig loaded with ordnance and munitions of war destined for the army in Boston. Two thousand stands of arms, several brass field-pieces, and a thirteen-inch mortar are among the trophies; and when they arrived in Cambridge Old Put, mounting the mortar, broke a bottle of rum over it, christening it the "Congress," amid deafening huzzas.

Here is what a British letter-writer says about this most fortunate capture: —

"This brig, whose safe arrival was of the utmost consequence to us, and whose cargo was of most infinite importance to the rebels, because she contained the very things they were in the greatest need of, and could not be supplied with by any other possible means, was sent from England with other artillery ships, and she the only one of them without a soldier on board, and totally unprovided with any means of defence. 'T is said they sailed under convoy of the 'Phœnix,' man-of-war, who quitted them a few days after they left the land.

"As they are now enabled to burn Boston, I most sincerely hope they will do it, that we may be enabled to leave it, and transfer the scene to some other part of the continent."

The Americans are now in great good humor. It is true, they say, that we have no arsenals, but the enemy has, and he will furnish what we need.

But Washington has thought of another way to procure cannon. The fortresses of Ticonderoga and Crown Point, which now belong to the Americans, are well furnished. The removal of a part of their armament to Cambridge has been constantly talked of. Now it is to be done. Washington looked around him for the man to do it, and his choice fell upon Henry Knox, who, with an instinct that it is his proper field, has zealously taken up the artillery branch of the service. So Knox is now on his way to Lake Champlain to get the battering train.

Meanwhile the General receives many guests, both civilians and military men, at headquarters. Mrs. Washington presides with dignified grace at the General's table, which custom requires the ladies to leave when the gentlemen begin their wine. The duty of introducing these guests — for General Washington insists upon the observance of proper etiquette — is performed by young Trumbull,[1] his aide-de-camp.

[1] Afterwards the celebrated painter. He attracted Washington's notice while serving as adjutant of Spencer's Connecticut regiment, by creeping near enough to the enemy's lines to make a drawing of them.

None of these guests is more honored, and none listened to with such respectful attention, as our Boston boy, Benjamin Franklin, who has come up from Philadelphia to look into the state of the army. He is now an old man, but the simple frugality of his life has strengthened a naturally robust constitution, so that many years of honorable service are yet in store for him. When he speaks, the young officers, who have been asked to meet him, hang upon his words with the closest attention.

FLAG OF THE BODYGUARD.

This is the man who singly faced the assembled British Lords of Council without flinching; who bore the sarcasms and abuse of the solicitor-general with perfect equanimity, while the noble lords laughed and cheered when that dignitary called him a thief in Latin, for having exposed the double-dealing of Governor Hutchinson. Let those laugh who win. They thought to crush Franklin; but though of humble origin, he was the peer of all those titled blackguards.

The man here who commands greater interest, perhaps, than almost any of the superior officers is General Charles Lee.

"A tall man, lank and thin, with a huge nose, a satirical mouth, and restless eyes, who sat his horse as if he had often ridden at fox-hunts in England, and wore his uniform with a cynical disregard of common opinion."

This is the portrait of Lee, a British colonel, living in America upon half-pay, who has espoused the patriot cause with impulsive ardor. Two of his fingers have been shot off in a duel. He has fought in Europe with distinction; he has lived and hunted among the Mohawk Indians, who admired him and made him a chief. A wild and adventurous life has been his. Now he has offered his sword to Congress, which looks upon him as a great accession to the cause. He is known to be capable and brave, and experienced officers are scarce.

But everything about this new general is singular, and he is therefore the object of much curiosity. Washington gives him command of the left wing. He takes possession of the Royall mansion, at Medford, christening it "Hobgoblin Hall." He is so careless of his dress as to give no clew to his rank; and wherever he goes, a big, shaggy, Pomeranian dog stalks at his heels, — even to the commander-in-chief's select levees. Spada is the dog's name. So great is Lee's attachment to this animal that people say of him, "Love me, love my dog."

General Lee is already a puzzle to his brother officers.

But everything is put down to eccentricity. It is plain that he is ambitious, but that is pardonable if it does not lead him too far. Doubtless he is a puzzle to himself: to friend or foe he may equally be a dangerous man.

General Gates, the new adjutant-general, is also become an important personage, as well from his confidential relation to the commander-in-chief, as for his duty to reorganize the army. He, too, was a retired English officer, living quietly upon his fine Virginia estate at the outbreak of the war. Now he is probably the hardest-worked man at Cambridge.

So the grave and sedate commander now has the support of a few educated military men in his great undertaking. The army is restive. Its spirit flags as the siege drags its slow length along. The men want to see their wives and little ones. When their short term of service expires they refuse to enlist again, and go home in large bodies. Perilous indeed is the situation of affairs while the army is being thus daily weakened. There are the miles of intrenchments, but where are the men to man them if attacked? Ah! should the enemy find out that they are defenceless! Rumor says that he does know this. Anxious days pass. A gloom hangs about headquarters, and is visible in the faces of all. What a chance for Sir William Howe! But he lets it slip by. The ghost of Bunker Hill waves him back. The British general has an army; the American has a few sentinels to personate one.

But the leader is always dauntless, always grand. If

he fears that all is over, nothing betrays it. It is only in the silence and darkness of that upper chamber that he unbosoms himself; and that no man sees. The Congress has made no mistake. True, its army has vanished, but the leader will find another. So trials, following trials, prove the wisdom of its choice. So may a single man be worth an army.[1]

[1] A laughable story, though belonging to a later period, is told of General Washington's headquarters. Samuel Breck is responsible for its appearance. When the first French squadron arrived in Boston, Nathaniel Tracy, who then lived in this house, gave a great banquet to the admiral and his officers. "Everything was furnished that could be had in the country to ornament and give variety to the entertainment. My father was one of the guests, and told me often after that two large tureens of soup were placed at the ends of the table. The admiral sat on the right of Tracy, and Monsieur de l'Etombe on the left. L'Etombe was consul of France, resident at Boston. Tracy filled a plate with soup, which went to the admiral, and the next was handed to the consul. As soon as l'Etombe put his spoon into his plate he fished up a large frog, just as green and perfect as if he had hopped from the pond into the tureen. Not knowing at first what it was, he seized it by one of its hind legs, and, holding it up in view of the whole company, discovered that it was a full-grown frog. As soon as he had thoroughly inspected it, and made himself sure of the matter, he exclaimed, 'Ah! mon Dieu! un grenouille!' then, turning to the gentleman next to him, gave him the frog. He received it and passed it round the table. Thus the poor crapaud made the tour from hand to hand until it reached the admiral. The company, convulsed with laughter, examined the soup-plates as the servants brought them, and in each was to be found a frog. The uproar was universal. 'What's the matter?' asked Tracy, raising his head and surveying the frogs dangling by a leg in all directions. 'Why don't they eat them? If they knew the con-

Somewhat farther down the Watertown road toward the college, on the opposite side, is the house once owned by Governor Belcher. This has lately been the prison of a traitor.

An intercepted letter, in cipher, disclosed the perfidy of a man who had hitherto been above suspicion. This was Dr. Benjamin Church, an early, and as all believed, one of the warmest of patriots. But his letter, intended for the enemy, condemned him. The commander-in-chief ordered his confinement in this house. Here let us leave him.[1]

Three or four more colonial estates invite us to continue our walk toward Watertown, where the Provincial Congress now sits. The first is that of Judge Sewall, the second that of Judge Lee, the third that of Mr. Fayerweather, and the fourth that of Lieutenant-Governor Oliver. These estates occupy all the ground between headquarters and the great bend of the road.[2] All are now deserted by their late occupants.

The lieutenant-governor, the judges Sewall and Lee,

founded trouble I had to catch them in order to treat them to a dish of their own country, they would find that with me, at least, it was no joking matter.'"

[1] This attractive colonial mansion is still standing, the grounds reaching to Ash Street. It was long the residence of the late Samuel Batchelder.

[2] That is, from Mr. Longfellow's to Mr. Lowell's. The old road did not go straight on by Mount Auburn, as at present, but passed by Governor Oliver's (Elmwood) house. All these houses are standing as I write.

were all compelled to resign and take refuge in Boston before open hostilities broke out. They and their friends formed the aristocratic coterie of Cambridge, which held

LIEUTENANT-GOVERNOR OLIVER'S.

its head as high as any in the land. This strip of road crossed an earthly paradise into which the serpent of civil strife has now entered.

Governor Oliver's has been taken for a hospital since the battle of Bunker Hill, the field opposite being used to bury such as have died of their wounds.

XVII.

TO ROXBURY TOWN.

RETURNING to the Common, we proceed directly to the bridge over the Charles, meaning now to pass over the road to Roxbury, viewing as we go the state of the defences and progress of the siege on that side.

Lord Percy had to cross this bridge on his way to Lexington. The inhabitants took up the planks; but not having secreted or destroyed them, his lordship passed his troops over, and so saved the first British detachment by joining them at the critical moment.

Expecting that he would return this way, the Americans a second time dismantled the bridge, this time using the planks to barricade the south end. A considerable number posted themselves behind the barricade, meaning to give the enemy a hot reception when he came.

Singularly enough, this was the first and only obstruction placed in the way of the enemy's advance and retreat during the 19th of April.

Instead of falling into the trap thus set for him, Lord Percy took the Charlestown road and so escaped. We say escaped because, with eight miles more of ambuscades to march through, his ammunition exhausted, and his men ready to drop from fatigue, the chance of reaching Boston this way was a desperate one. Probably not half his command would have succeeded in gaining the British lines.

When this strong reinforcement marched out of Boston neither officers nor men had the least idea that the Yankees were at that very moment driving their comrades in utter rout before them. So while one body marched slowly along with its usual insolent bearing, its music derisively playing Yankee Doodle, the other was approaching it on the run, shorn of all its pomp, deprived of its courage, — a mere mob of dirty, exhausted, and terrified fugitives. This day was pricked that impudent self-conceit with which the British army was so ridiculously inflated.

So the small boy who planted himself where he could see Percy's columns pass by, who cut up such queer antics, and who laughed so immoderately that the Earl rode up to inquire what he was laughing at, was a sort of prophet of evil.

"To think how you will dance by and by to the tune of Chevy Chase,"[1] cried the young rebel.

[1] Read the ancient English ballad for an explanation of this answer. It does seem rather deep for a boy, but is narrated by the historian Gordon.

Did this saucy country urchin possess the gift of second sight? and did he see the soldiers of the monarchy every moment biting the dust along the Lexington highway?

The brigade marches through Roxbury and takes the Cambridge road. Not a soul is anywhere to be seen. One would have thought the country suddenly depopulated. The road is abandoned, the houses shut up and deserted. An ominous silence reigns everywhere.

One long catalogue of blunders signalled the history of this ill-starred expedition. Let us number a few of them.

In the first place, General Gage confided his secret intention to some one who told it. The Americans were thus forewarned and alert.

In the second, the preparations were so faulty that the grenadiers and light-infantry stood for two hours waiting on the Cambridge marshes after landing there. These two hours gave time for the country to be thoroughly alarmed in advance of the troops. The intended surprise was therefore a signal failure.

In the third, a negligent officer only half executed the orders for Percy's brigade to get under arms in season for it to march at an early hour. Neglect and red-tape thus prevented the junction of Percy with Colonel Smith at Concord. Had that taken place, the British would then have been too strong to be driven like sheep.

In the fourth, Lord Percy's neglect to secure the bridge at Cambridge, over which he must pass, was the cause not only of delay, but the loss of his provisions and ammunition. The wagons containing them, having fallen behind the main body, were captured by our people. Having soon expended his cannon ammunition, the pieces were only so much old brass, and they impeded his rapid retreat; but a sentiment of honor obliges an army to save its cannon at all hazards. And as a certain portion of good luck always falls to the share of blunderers, the king's troops effected their retreat safely.

The Americans too, wanting a leader, wanting previous and concerted action, did not make the best use of their opportunities. After expecting this very movement so long, they were really disconcerted by it. They practised the irregular bush-fighting of the Indians with great effect; but they neither destroyed a bridge, felled a tree, or barricaded a road, except in the single instance mentioned.

As this was a conflict between squads or individuals there were many trials of individual courage. A Briton and American met by the roadside. The first, levelling his musket, said: —

"You are a dead man!"

"You are another!" his adversary exclaimed, covering his enemy with fatal aim.

Both fired at the same instant. Both fell.

Another desperate encounter, that will long be told at the family fireside, was the duel between Eliphalet Downer of Punch-Bowl Village[1] and a grenadier. The soldier had stopped to pillage a house when he and the minuteman saw each other. Both fired at the same instant and both missed. They then closed in deadly struggle with the bayonet. But Downer soon found he was no match for his antagonist with this weapon. Seconds must decide. Collecting all his strength for a decisive effort, he suddenly reversed his firelock, and dealing the Briton a terrific blow on the head with the butt, brought him to the ground. He then finished him with the cold steel.

This "great bridge," as it was long called, which we have now crossed, was one of the first ever built in the colony, and before its day a ferryman conveyed people to and fro.[2]

This, too, is the great highway between Boston and the interior, particularly the western and southwestern portions of New England, by which reinforcements, munitions, and provisions must arrive for the army. It is now also an important military road traversing the American lines, and as such must be strictly maintained. If the British can land a force and get possession of this road somewhere between Cambridge and Roxbury, they can cut off one part of the investing army from the other. If they

---

[1] A precinct of Brookline formerly so called from the Punch Bowl Tavern, a famous resort in its day.

[2] Brighton was then a part of Cambridge, called Little Cambridge in the Revolutionary time.

can hold it they can compel Washington to raise the
siege.

The General expects this; for the enemy's boats constantly patrol the river, and he keeps one or two ships of war well up the channel. The boats are seen taking soundings, while the ships are kept ready for action. By and by the broad basin here will be solidly frozen so that the river will form a bridge over which troops may march as easily as on the land.

In order to protect his camps at Cambridge and his communication with Roxbury, Washington has caused the erection of redoubts on each side of the Charles, near its mouth.[1] These will effectually stop the enemy from going up the river. But a still better thing is going to be done. The enemy's vessels are to be driven out of the river altogether.

Our progress towards Roxbury is not to be delayed by anything more important than the movement of small bodies of soldiers, — probably recruits going to join the army, — ox-carts and wagons impressed for the transportation of supplies from the inland towns, — for Washington's army is mainly fed by requisitions upon the towns for so much flour, beef, pease, hay, etc., — droves of cattle or sheep, grimy laborers repairing the roadway, and exchanging a jest or a scrap of camp news with the wagoners or

---

[1] These forts were a short distance above the bridge now connecting Brookline and Cambridgeport.

drovers, or a cavalcade of officers going the rounds from post to post.

About a mile south of the bridge we pass the house of Colonel Thomas Gardner, one of the fallen heroes of Bunker Hill. He fell mortally wounded while leading a portion of his regiment from Bunker Hill up to the redoubt at the most critical moment of the day. His son, a youth of nineteen, wished to assist his wounded parent from the field of carnage, but the father — stern old Roman that he was — ordered the lad to remain and do his duty in the battle.[1]

Borne from the field upon a rude litter, the expiring hero could yet speak cheering words to the soldiers whom the dreadful scenes of the day had unnerved. One of the very first orders Washington published to his army was a tribute of respect to this gallant soldier, who was buried with military honors by command of the beloved chief.

The district through which we are passing is wholly devoted to farms. The houses, except near the village centres, are quite unfrequent and of the antiquated pattern seen everywhere in the country. They are certainly very humble-looking; but to defend them the stout Middlesex yeomanry have taken their old Queen's arms and gone to camp, followed by the blessings of wives, mothers, and sweethearts.

[1] The house of Jesse Turell now occupies the site of Colonel Gardner's, that having been removed to Allston Street.

XVIII.

ROXBURY CAMP AND LINES.

AT the left of the road, just before descending Parker Hill into the thickly settled part of Roxbury, we come to the comfortable country-seat of the Brinleys, a family of note in the Province. Although now the property of Robert Pierpont, a Boston merchant, this mansion is still known as Colonel Brinley's.

Since being assigned to the command of the right of the army, General Artemas Ward has fixed his headquarters in this house.[1] Near by is the noble eminence of Parker Hill, on which several regiments have pitched their tents; while just beyond us rise the formidable and precipitous rocks, forming the Americans' second line by a chain of forts and redoubts of great natural and artificial strength. Indeed, as we examine it from this spot, the crest of the next high hill seems unassailable. A cluster of naked gray rock, showing here and there a huge boulder, stopped in its descent, rises above the thickets surround-

[1] This house stood next to the fine cathedral of the Redemptorists which now occupies the old estate.

ing its base. This has been fortified with great labor and skill. If driven from all other posts, the Americans will hold this one to the last.

Leaving General Ward's, we come to houses scattered along the road where it crosses Stony Brook. From a

HIGH FORT, ROXBURY.

very early time there has been a mill here, around which these houses have collected. The place is now called Pierpont's Village, from the ancient mill-owner of that name.[1]

Beginning now to ascend towards the heights we have just seen from the road, we pass first the Workhouse on our right, then a large earthwork on our left, built at the intersection of the Cambridge with the Dedham and Rhode Island road. This work covers these important highways.

Pause a moment here, — long enough to read the in-

[1] Pierpont's Village now coincides with the junction of Tremont and Roxbury Streets.

scription upon this stone placed at the junction, or rather parting of these roads. From this circumstance it is called the "Parting Stone," and is a well-known point of direction to all travellers. In common parlance it is a mile-stone. One side directs to Cambridge and Watertown, the other to Dedham and Rhode Island. The tired wayfarer may sit and rest upon it ere he takes the hot road again. And perhaps the honorable Paul Dudley, whose name is cut at the bottom, may have thought of this use when placing the stone here. If so it was a kind act.

THE PARTING STONE.

It is said that a certain Duke of Argyle once placed posts upon the public ways for his brother Scotsmen to rub themselves, pig-like, against. When Sandy came to one of these posts he would fervently exclaim, "God bless the Duke of Argyle!" But this is much better done. Let us thank Paul Dudley, and kindly commit his gift to the care of future generations.

But we are at length arrived within the limits of another large military encampment, denoting the presence of a considerable force. Right before us, in the centre of the hill, rises Roxbury Meeting-House, on the spot where that great and good man, John Eliot, preached so long ago. This, then, is Meeting-House Hill.

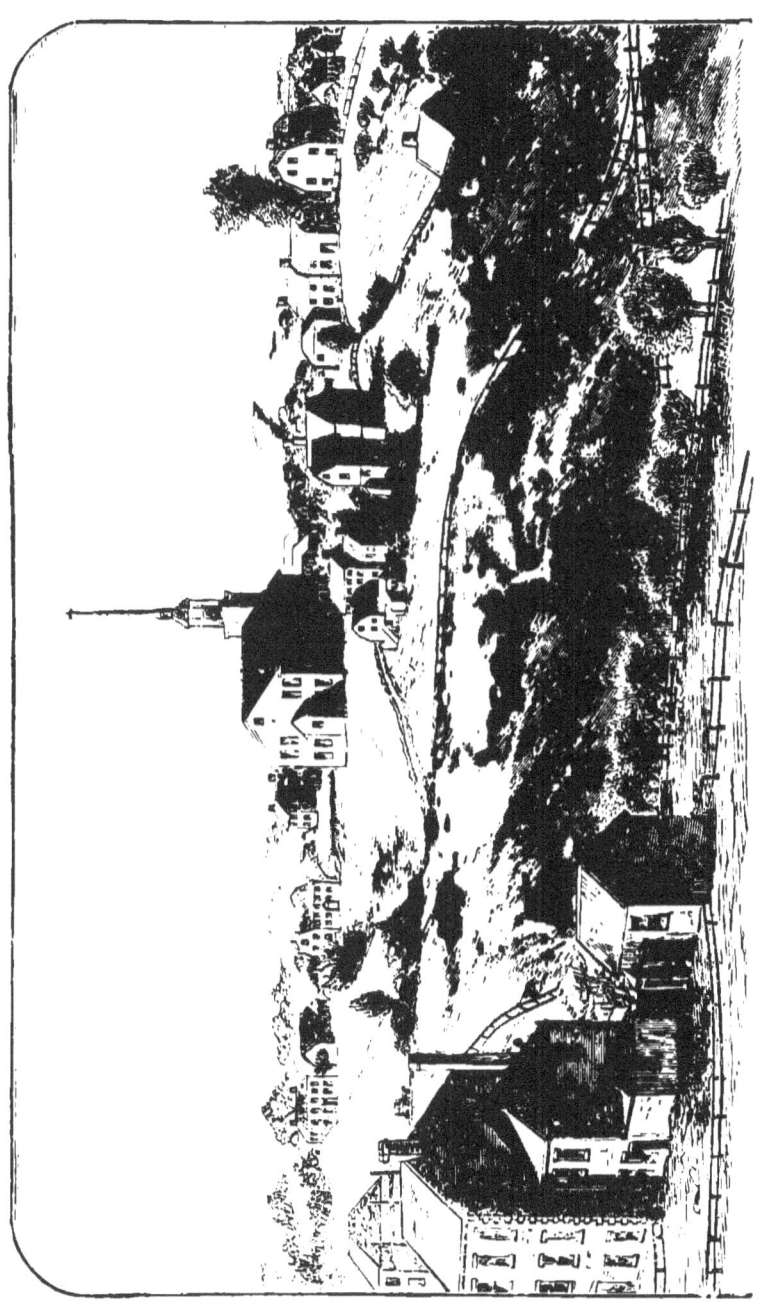

MEETING-HOUSE HILL, ROXBURY, 1790.

THE PARSONAGE.

This too is the principal post of General Ward's command. It is a much cooler and more inviting spot than Cambridge Common, being reached by the breezes from the bay. From the camps here all Boston may be seen, and any demonstration made by the enemy instantly detected and provided against.

So that when the militia swarmed like angry bees after the battle of Lexington, they pitched their bivouacs upon this commanding hill; but in a few days the greater portion left for home as suddenly as they came. True, they could not be greatly blamed for doing so, for they had marched at a moment's notice under the impulse of fierce excitement. The officers saw this wholesale desertion with great apprehension, but without the power to prevent it. One of them Colonel Lemuel Robinson, was ordered to hold this position with only six or seven hundred men. Now it is one thing to order and another to perform. He had no officers to assist him, he had nine miles of country to patrol and guard; yet upon his vigilance everything depended. For nine days and nights the Colonel never took off his clothes or lay down to sleep.

General John Thomas took the command here until relieved by General Ward. Since then he is his most trusted officer, but acting now under his commission of brigadier from the Continental Congress. His camp is the healthiest and most orderly of any. He is a very cool, sagacious, and brave officer, experienced in war and wise in council. From him Massachusetts expects as much, perhaps, as from any man she has sent into the field, since the lamented Warren's death. He occupies the parsonage as his headquarters.

A man of ready wit, too, is General John Thomas. Hearing that General Gage means to come out and attack him, and having only seven hundred men, he hits upon this clever trick of war. The brow of the hill is in plain view from the British lines. In order to deceive the enemy as to his real weakness, he kept his seven hundred men marching for several hours around the hill, so as to give the appearance of large bodies of troops arriving and manœuvring. Time was thus gained, when time was everything.

From Meeting-House Hill, back of it, lifts the high rocky eminence we first descried when approaching by the Cambridge road. The Americans are still busy as bees strengthening it and placing heavy cannon in position. This is usually called Roxbury High Fort, and by some it is called the "Upper Fort," to distinguish it from the one lower down and nearer to us. It was at the troops encamped here, on Meeting-House Hill, that the enemy directed his cannonade on the 17th of June. This was done to prevent the sending of any troops from Roxbury to reinforce their comrades in the battle. From the upper windows of General Thomas's headquarters Charlestown is in full view, but the distance is too great for the spectators of that day to distinguish with the naked eye how the battle was going. The anxiety was, on this account, all the greater. The Connecticut troops, then occupying the ground between the meeting-house and the road, could not stand Lord Percy's fire and they could not return it; so they had to fall back to the summit of the hill behind them, where they lay all night on their arms, expecting an attack every hour.

The adjutant of Spencer's regiment has kindly preserved for us the following particulars of that night of dread:—

"Charlestown, which lay full in our view, was one extended line of fire. The British were apparently apprehensive that their obstinate enemy might rally and renew the action, and therefore kept up during the night a frequent fire of shot and shells in the direction of Cambridge. The roar of artillery, the bursting of shells (whose track, like that of a comet, was marked on the dark sky by a long train of light from the burning fuse), and the blazing ruins of the town, formed altogether a sublime scene of military magnificence and ruin. That night was a fearful breaking-in for young soldiers, who there for the first time were seeking repose on the summit of a bare rock surrounded by such a scene."

When he spoke of young soldiers Adjutant Trumbull was no doubt thinking of himself, for he was not quite twenty years of age when on this day he for the first time saw men falling under the enemy's fire within reach of his arm.[1]

We first have leave to inspect the lower fort, which is

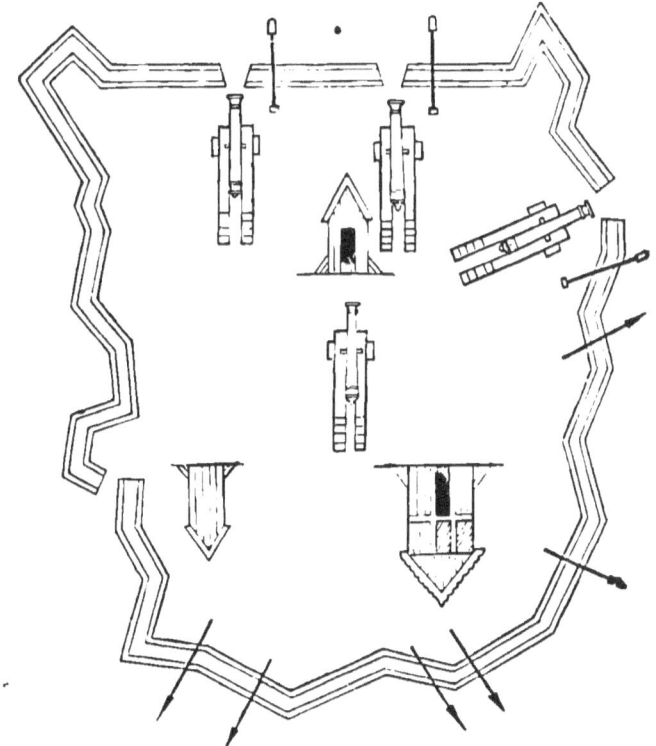

ROXBURY FORT FROM A POWDER-HORN.

[1] Trumbull, after the war was over, painted his great historical picture of the battle of Bunker Hill in London, in the studio of Benjamin West. Some of the British officers who had fought in the battle sat to him for their portraits.

very eligibly located about two hundred yards above the meeting-house.[1] The hill-top is in some places so bare of soil that earth to form the ramparts had to be taken where it could be found. About two acres are enclosed by its walls, which zig-zag according to the configuration of the rock on which the fort stands. Two twenty-four pounders have been dragged up the hill and placed in position.

The soldiers love to ornament their powder-horns with carvings, some of which are very skilfully done. In this way they preserve a sort of record of their campaigns, as the Indians did. One has thus engraved upon his horn a ground-plan of this very fortification, showing, besides the cannon, the lances kept ready to repel an assault. These lances, or spears, are well greased, so that an enemy cannot grasp them, reminding one of the boarding-pikes used in naval combats. They answer very well in room of bayonets, and General Ward says that if our men at Breed's Hill had been provided with them they would have held their ground.

The high fort, which we first observed, lies back of this one and overlooks it. It would not do, therefore, to leave so commanding a position unguarded.

With these works the Americans now threaten the enemy, should he attempt to advance from his lines on Boston Neck, and they at the same time cover the roads to

---

[1] Near the junction of Highland with Cedar Street, and partly upon the beautiful estate of N. J. Bradlee.

Cambridge, Dedham, and Dorchester. General Thomas's pickets are thrown well out on the Neck, his advanced post being at the George Tavern. So far, on this side as well as on that of Charlestown, the Americans have been satisfied to maintain a blockade by land, without attempting to drive the enemy out. They have not yet the means.

Of course, seeing these works going on, the British tried to stop them by firing at the workmen. Our raw soldiers were at first so much terrified by the screaming of shot and explosion of bombs that they would drop their tools and run helter-skelter for the nearest shelter. To render them more courageous a reward was offered in general orders for every cannon-ball picked up and brought to headquarters. This had the effect desired. The men, when they saw a ball strike, and then rebound and skip along the ground, would run after it with all the eagerness of school-boys playing at a favorite game. If it was a shell, they would snatch the burning fuse away. But, after all, the order proved an unfortunate one, for several soldiers had their feet badly crushed while trying to stop a ball which seemed to be slowly rolling along, but had not quite spent its force. So this dangerous game of foot-ball was discontinued.

Having seen all that we may in this region, let us now descend the hill on the side opposite to that by which we came, taking a look over the Neck, which has become a sort of duelling-ground for the advanced guards of both armies, because if one side undertakes to do a bold thing the other tries to counteract it with a bolder.

At the foot of the hill we find the old, time-honored estate of the Dudleys,[1] covered with intrenchments, for military necessity respects neither the living nor the dead, and this house stood where the roads to Dorchester and Cambridge divide. It is also a sort of outwork to the forts we have just visited on the heights; it has, therefore, a strategic importance.

The old mansion was demolished a few days after the battle of Bunker Hill, the brick walls of the basement now forming the northeast angle of the fortification. So good-by to the sturdy old governor's New England home and to all the Dudleys who have since lived here in state. Perhaps it is less respected that its latest inhabitant, Isaac Winslow, farmer, is a Tory refugee in Boston.

It would not take us much out of our way were we now to ascend the upper road to Dorchester as far as the old farm-house on the left in which that noble young martyr to the patriot cause, General Joseph Warren, was born.[2] The house is now, however, in the occupation of the Provincial infantry. It is simply a substantial, unpretending dwelling, like the hundreds we have already seen, and which all seem the work of one builder.

But let us hasten on until we reach the old burial-

---

[1] The Universalist Church now stands on the spot.
[2] This house was on Warren Street. Its site is now marked by a stone dwelling with appropriate tablets in the walls.

ground in which the ashes of Eliot and the Dudleys mingle with the dust.

We now find it to be true that in war neither the abodes of the living nor the dead can be spared. For right here

THE WARREN HOMESTEAD.

the Americans have carried an earthwork quite across the highway, while beyond, toward Boston, it is still further obstructed by trees that have been cut down for the purpose. This is the "Burying-Ground Redoubt." Those trees are to stop the British cavalry from riding out some morning with drawn sabres to pay us a visit. Along the highway we see the ruins of houses pulled down to prevent their being occupied by the enemy and to give the gunners a clear view of the Neck; and we further note that the houses in this vicinity show every now and then a shot-hole, a tottering chimney-stack, windows with not a whole pane of glass remaining, or walls shattered or split by bursting shells; now and then one has been set on fire and half consumed before it could be extinguished.

So that by the hand of friend and foe — for war makes no distinction here — the peaceful homes of Christian people are given up to destruction. The regulars, who send their shot red-hot from the furnace among these dwellings, feel no compunction, — not they. They do not care whom or how many they may render houseless or homeless. Yesterday it was Charlestown, to-day it is Roxbury; and to-morrow, it may be, some other thriving town will be given to the flames. But the Americans care. They are fighting now for their hearthstones. The regular is fighting for sixpence a day.

By going as far as our pickets, who are posted on the high ground at the George Tavern, we plainly descry the strong works erected by the enemy some distance in front of the old fortifications. A formidable array of cannon glistens on the ramparts. His picket-post is at Enoch Brown's chimneys. The houses are no longer there.

A night or two ago the two great guns at the high fort drove their shot into the British works, causing the picket to leave their post in a hurry. Our people were not disposed to let the enemy hold so advanced a position at Brown's, from which he might make a dash at our lines.

We hear that two Americans, who volunteered to go down and set fire to Brown's house, store, and barn, were killed in the attempt. They went boldly toward the enemy, and even reached the houses, but, being discovered, and thought to be deserters coming in to give themselves up, a party came out of the works to meet them. Upon their approach the two Americans fired and then retreated, but were instantly saluted with a volley by which both were killed.

This little exploit only rendered the Americans still more determined to accomplish their purpose. It rendered the British insolent, for at daybreak on the following morning they came up and fired on our sentinels at the tavern. Our people returned the compliment, when the regulars ran off, as our lads jestingly say, "without paying their score."

These houses were, however, no longer to serve the enemy as a place to skulk in.

On the evening of the 8th of July two hundred men were quietly got under arms. They belonged to Rhode Island and Massachusetts regiments, and were commanded by the gallant Tupper and the brave Crane. At ten o'clock six picked men made their way across the marsh to the rear of the guard-house occupied by the enemy. The rest concealed themselves in the marsh, on both sides of the

Neck, at about two hundred yards from the house. Two small cannon were also quietly brought to the spot. As soon as the six pioneers gained the desired position, they gave the signal agreed upon, when two rounds of cannon-shot instantly crashed through the guard-house. The British guard of forty-five or fifty men did not wait for a second discharge, but were saluted as they came out by a tremendous volley of small arms. The six men then set the house on fire, and it was burned to the ground.[1]

Thus here on the Neck the officers on both sides are continually planning how they may do each other the most mischief. It is tit for tat, blow for blow, shot for shot.

Occasionally an officer of one side or the other goes out from the advanced post waving a white handkerchief on the point of his sword. He thus signifies a desire for an interview, or in the military phrase, a "parley." Then, at sight of this little square of cloth, all firing stops; then the men, who just now were scheming how they could kill or disable each other, meet under this banner of peace — a flag of truce — like old friends. They shake hands, joke, and banter each other. Having despatched the business which brought them together, they no sooner gain the shelter of their own works than they again begin shooting at each other in cold blood.

---

[1] The British soon, however, retaliated by setting fire to and destroying the George Tavern. This gallant feat was performed by Captain Evelyn of the King's Own.

XIX.

ORDERS OF THE DAY.

THE dreary winter has passed away, and still the hostile armies remain confronting each other as they have done ever since the 19th of April.

Washington has kept his army busy intrenching. On his left, Cobble Hill and Lechmere's Point have been heaped with earthworks, which have driven the enemy's shipping out of the Charles. On his right, the Roxbury lines are advanced as far as the George Tavern; and on his extreme right, he has thrown up works at the Five Corners commanding the road to Dorchester Neck.

But behind these miles of intrenchments his first army has melted away, and he has been obliged to form another, with an enemy ready and waiting to take advantage of his weakness. These are anxious days for the General; these are critical hours for America.

At last! At last the army is again strong. At last our frowning batteries bid the enemy defiance. At last the cannon have come.

Yes, on a train of sleds Knox has at last brought all those guns and mortars from Lake Champlain. On the 24th of January they arrive in camp. From this day the real siege begins.

For this gallant exploit Washington hands Knox his commission as colonel of artillery. As fast as possible the cannon and the mortars are put in position. The bare earthen walls begin to show their teeth. All through the month of February the greatest activity prevails in the American encampments. This army is at last getting ready to fight.

All the heights around Boston are now included in the American line of investment, except those of Dorchester, which command both the town and the harbor. It is finally determined at headquarters to seize and fortify these.

Let us now turn over a few of the orders issued from headquarters during these momentous days: —

"HEADQUARTERS, Feb. 27, 1776.

"Parole HANCOCK, Countersign ADAMS. [Extract.] As the season is now fast approaching when every man must expect to be drawn into the field of action, it is highly necessary that he should prepare his mind as well as every necessary for it. It is a noble cause we are engaged in: it is the cause of virtue and mankind. Every temporal advantage to us and our posterity depends on the vigor of our exertions. In short, freedom or slavery must be the result of our conduct. There can, therefore, be no greater inducement for men to behave well; but it may not be amiss for the troops to know that if any man in action shall presume to skulk, or hide himself, or retreat from the enemy without the order of his commanding officer, he will be instantly shot down as an example of cowardice."

Washington has informed the Provincial Congress of his intention, and that body has ordered the militia in from the country to take part in the closing scenes. For Washington rightly concludes that his movement upon Dorchester will either bring on a general action or drive the enemy from Boston. He has fully determined to make an end of the siege. With this view he has formed four thousand men, at Cambridge, into a picked corps, under the command of General Putnam. Now, if the British attack him in force at Dorchester, these four thousand men will embark in boats, prepared for the purpose, and attack on the west side of Boston.

The night of the 2d of March comes. All is quiet. But the American cannoneers, standing motionless around their guns, are waiting for something. From the rocky and mounded heights, shrouded in thick darkness, they see the lights of the beleaguered town dimly twinkling in the distance. The inhabitants, suspecting nothing, are in their beds. Mothers clasp their babes to their hearts. Watchmen nod and sentinels yawn in the streets. Confiding in Heaven, the town goes fast asleep.

One hour before midnight the watchers on the American ramparts see the flash and hear the boom of a single gun. It is the signal. In an instant the heavens are lighted with the flashes of a hundred fiery mouths. The deadly missiles go crashing among the houses as if each had its separate errand of destruction. Startled from their peaceful slumbers, the people rush frantically into the streets. Many believe the Judgment Day has come. Soon the enemy's batteries reply, and until daybreak from shore to shore the iron tempest falls unceasingly.

We will now turn another leaf : —

"HEADQUARTERS, March 3, 1776.

"[Extract.] Two companies of Colonel Thomson's rifle regiment are to march to-morrow evening to Roxbury with their blankets, arms, and three days' provisions ready dressed. The officer commanding will receive his orders from the adjutant-general. Colonel Hutchinson's and Colonel French's regiments are to march to Roxbury by sunrise on Tuesday morning, with their blankets, arms, and three days' provisions ready dressed."

This night the bombardment is resumed with greater fury than ever. Bundles of screwed hay, fascines, and intrenching tools have been collected in vast numbers at Roxbury. The surgeons have made a great store of lint, bandages, and stretchers for the wounded. The engineers have also prepared and have in readiness a quantity of chandeliers or planks having an upright picket at each end. The country round has been swept clean of carts to carry all this material to Dorchester.

On the 4th Roxbury presents a scene of activity and bustle. The streets and camps look as if it had been raining men. Everything is ready. The militia have come in in swarms to take the places of the troops who are to meet the enemy in the field. Spears are sharpened, powder and ball served out, canteens filled, arms carefully inspected, and, as is usual in moments of intense expectation, every one is anxious to put an end to the suspense.

General Washington understands that imagination exerts a powerful effect upon soldiers. If he can arouse their enthusiasm by some appeal to their feelings they will fight all the better for it. He and his council having first decided to offer battle, next considered what day to fix upon for the purpose. They settled upon the 5th of March, — the day of the Boston Massacre.

This is the last general order preceding the movement upon Dorchester: —

"HEADQUARTERS, March 4, 1776.

"The flag on Prospect Hill and that at the Laboratory on Cambridge Common are to be hoisted only upon a general alarum; of this the whole army is to take particular notice, and immediately upon those colors being displayed, every officer and soldier must repair to his alarum post. This to remain a standing order until the Commander-in-chief shall please to direct otherwise."

XX.

THE SPIRIT OF SEVENTY-SIX.

AT sunset, the hour for which thousands have so eagerly waited, the suppressed excitement in the camps at Roxbury breaks forth. At the first tap of the drum armed men spring from the ground, battalions muster, columns form. A feverish excitement marks the importance of the hour. The long train of wagons moves out on the frozen road. The drivers speak to their animals in low voices; the officers give the word of command in whispers.

Darkness quickly settles down over the scene. Now forward! A darkly moving mass advances at a quick step along the Dorchester road. This is the vanguard of eight hundred men. No huzzas, no disorder, nothing but that muffled and solid tread on the frozen road. Their comrades look on in silence as they move silently by. Now three hundred wagons, loaded with fascines, hay, and intrenching tools, follow the vanguard. Soon they too are swallowed up in the darkness. Now that long line, stretching a wall of black up the hillside, suddenly detaching itself, is put in motion. One, two, three, four strong battalions tramp by. Each dusky face is set and determined. Now they are gone. Two thousand four hundred Continentals are moving at the will of one man to seize Dorchester Heights. That one man is General Washington.

GOVERNOR SHIRLEY'S MANSION.

Nothing that human foresight can supply has been forgotten. The men know this; they know that they will not be compelled, after toiling all night with the spade, to fight all the next day with the musket. There is discipline and there is the confidence of leadership. The mistakes of Bunker Hill will not be repeated here.

The long procession, on its way, marches past the fine old mansion of Governor Shirley, who built it; but the fate of many of the palatial colonial residences — and this is one of the grandest — has also overtaken this one; for having passed out of the governor's hands into the possession of his son-in-law, Judge Eliakim Hutchinson, it is now, as the estate of a Tory, held by the Provincial Government, and appropriated to military uses. It is now a barrack. Colonel Whitcomb's regiment occupies the house and grounds as an advanced post toward the Dorchester lines and for the security of these lines. That regiment has already joined these troops detailed for the work of to-night.

Seven o'clock. The front has now arrived at the lines at the Five Corners, beyond which there is only a long and narrow causeway leading to the Neck and to the Heights. Here a halt is ordered.

In the angle of the roads here stands the house of Mr. Commissioner Burch,[1] an officer of his Majesty's customs, and a stanch Loyalist. This proprietor, too, has fled, and his house is now a barrack, most conveniently situated at the extreme outpost of the Americans. To think of that ragamuffin soldiery cutting their meat on his mahogany tables with their swords, and prodding his ceilings with their bayonets, is enough to make the owner foam with rage.

Without leaving their ranks the troops wait here for

[1] Like the Shirley mansion, this house is also still standing. It is the birthplace of Edward Everett.

orders. As the moon rises, its light threatens discovery, but fortunately a cold haze, settling over the land and water, renders the column invisible to the enemy's sentinels. Fortune thus favors the Americans, for the causeway over which they must now pass is enfiladed by the British cannon on Boston Neck. But this too has been provided for. Let us walk on.

The bundles of hay are now being unloaded and placed along that side of the causeway next to the enemy, thus forming a protection behind which the troops may defile in safety. This is soon effected. The enemy's batteries remain silent.

Suddenly, at half-past seven, fire streams from an American battery in Roxbury. The bombardment begins anew as on the preceding nights, only this time it is a signal and a blind,—a signal to General Thomas to march boldly on, a blind to hide that march from the enemy.

And General Thomas — for it is he who commands the expedition — once more puts his columns in motion to the sound of the cannon. If they pass unperceived, they are safe.

The troops, startled and excited by the incessant explosions and the deafening roar of artillery around them, push on across the long and narrow causeway to the firm ground opposite. Thus far all is well. In places where the carts have become tightly wedged in the road, the soldiers are obliged to turn out and take to the marshes. At length all are crossed.

Here the advanced guard, dividing in two columns, is pushed forward, one to the farthest seaward point of the neck, opposite to which Castle William rises darkly out of the sea, one to the shore nearest to the town of Boston. They thus form two strong guards watching the least movement of the enemy.

At the same time Thomas leads the main body directly up the heights, which have two commanding eminences. The engineers lay out the works, the pickets are driven, the intrenching materials are unloaded, and the men, piling their arms, begin to break the solid crust of the earth with their sturdy blows.

The ground is hard frozen to the depth of eighteen inches. To throw up earthworks with rapidity is therefore out of the question. But this too has been foreseen. In the American camp there is an ingenious officer named Rufus Putnam. Before the war he was a millwright, now he is one of the best engineers in the army. He has planned a novel way to build these forts. All these materials — hay, fascines, chandeliers — have been provided for this very contingency. The men now lay the chandeliers along the ground, marking the line of the works at proper distances. They soon have a double line of pickets, three feet apart, enclosing the ground. The fascines are then piled within these pickets, and in one hour two forts, one on each high hill, forming a sufficient protection against musketry, are thus completed. The working parties continue to deepen the ditches and strengthen the parapet until day breaks.[1]

While this is going on other parties have been busy cutting down the adjoining orchards, and placing the trees in rows around the works, the branches outward, the more effectually to stop an enemy.[2] And a still more novel method of carrying destruction into the enemy's ranks, should he venture to assault, has been devised. Barrels, filled with earth, are placed all around the works as if to strengthen them, but they are really meant to be rolled down the steep hillside with tremendous velocity upon the heads of the storming columns, at the critical moment.

So far everything has succeeded admirably, because nothing has been left to chance. Promptly at dawn three thousand fresh men cross over from Roxbury to relieve their comrades. The men who have built the forts resign them to these reinforcements, and, resuming their arms, march back to their camps without a scratch, but weary and hungry with their night of incessant toil.

But the master-spirit, where is he during the anxious hours of this night? Shall we seek him at Cambridge, snatching a little fitful slumber amid the din of cannon and screaming of bombs? Will he be content to wholly resign the work of to-night to his lieutenants? Not he: his is the master mind, they are but the arm.

[1] Four smaller forts were also built the same night.
[2] This is called an *abatis*.

The weary wagoner, returning from his night of toil, sees a cloaked figure emerge from the obscurity before him. As it passes like the wind he holds for one instant the strong and well-known features of the head of the army.

Now, Sir William Howe, if you keep Boston you must fight for it. The Virginian whom you and your officers have ridiculed so long is thundering at your doors.

For once Fortune, that fickle one, is on the side of America. Even Nature lends her aid to give victory to the sons of New England. For while they still labor in the trenches on the hill-tops in the clear sunshine of open day, the same thick haze overspreads everything below, so that their enemies do not see them until the Yankee lads are ready.

As the sun slowly disperses the mists Washington's picked battalions stand to their arms, eagerly watching the town. Discovery is now certain. What will the British do?

At length the drowsy sentinels espy the intrenchments looming in the distance. They rub their eyes. Astonishment and consternation are in every face. Turn out the guards! Beat drums! Blow bugles! Up and arm! Once more Young America dares Old England to the field. The unwelcome news is carried in haste to General Howe, who looks long and fixedly at the American forts, then shuts his glass, saying: —

"Those rebels have done more in one night than my whole army would have done in months."

He has hardly time to turn over in his mind what he will do to save his own and his king's credit, before a messenger comes from the admiral of the fleet to tell him that if the Americans are permitted to remain on those heights they will sink every one of his Majesty's ships in the harbor. And to prevent such disaster he, the admiral, must take them out of harm's way.

Lieutenant-General Sir William Howe can always be depended on to fight. That is his reputation. That is now his determination. His council meets to consider which of two alternatives they will choose, — leave the town or storm the heights. In reality these alternatives are not submitted to the council by General Howe, but by General Washington. He is master of this situation.

"Make your enemy do the thing he does not wish to do" is a maxim of war. General Howe's resolution exactly agrees with Washington's hopes. In truth, the chances are five to one against the British. Still, British honor is at stake. "What will they say of us in England?" is in Sir William's mind.

The enemy's council decides upon a double attack, as at Bunker Hill. Five regiments are ordered on board transport vessels. These are destined to be landed near the Castle under cover of the broadsides of the ships of war. The grenadiers, light-infantry, and other troops, numbering, all told, perhaps two thousand more, are to land nearer the causeway. The order is not to let the men load at all, but rely on a rush with the bayonet.

General Howe has also learned something at Bunker Hill. He will put one column where it will cut off retreat if his assault succeeds. He will not let his troops keep up a harmless popping at the intrenchments while being picked off at the rate of a company a minute.

Earl Percy, who won his spurs at the Lexington races, is to command the assaulting columns. Brigadier Jones supports him.

Again, as on the fatal 17th of June, all is hurry, all is bustle, in Boston. The inhabitants run to and fro. If patriots, they are flushed and elated at the near prospect of rescue from British tyranny; for General Howe has ruled them with a rod of iron. If Tories, they are in despair at the thought of becoming exiles from their native land; for the patriots detest them even more than they hate the soldiers. The soldiers, ordered out for the expedition, form in the streets in front of their barracks. They look pale and dejected. Here and there one, while nervously fixing and unfixing his bayonet, mutters to himself: —

"Another Bunker Hill — or worse."

As these troops march through the streets to the wharves, the Americans on the heights, thinking they are to attack them immediately, clap their hands, round after round. "Let them come!" is the cry. Very different is the spirit animating the men who to-day are to shed their blood for king or country. One would not think these spectators were so soon to close in deadly combat.

Upon this movement of the enemy the news flies from Dorchester to Roxbury and from Roxbury to Cambridge. Twenty thousand freemen spring to arms. Putnam, Greene, and Stark muster their veteran battalions. The surrounding hills are alive with spectators.

At that moment Washington believes the decisive hour is about to strike. Turning to those soldiers nearest him he says: —

"Remember the 5th of March, and avenge your brethren!"

Those who are not near enough to hear eagerly ask what the General is saying. His words are passed along the lines of steel.

"Remember the 5th of March!"

Already excited by the scenes around them, — the grandeur of the arena, the plaudits of the spectators, — this exhortation adds fuel to the flame. It becomes the battle-cry repeated from a thousand throats. Swords flash, standards wave, eyes sparkle with martial fire, while the noble determination to conquer or die burns brightly in every breast.

But the struggle is not to be. Indeed, Sir William does not mean to attack before to-morrow. The Americans, standing to their arms in grim expectation, watch the tide go down until late in the afternoon, when it become impracticable for boats to approach the shore, as the flats here extend far out into the harbor.

So the 5th passes. Late in the day the transports with a floating battery drop down to the Castle. But there is no vigor about Sir William's preparations. The night brings a hurricane of great violence, which dashes three of the vessels on the rocks of Governor's Island. The storm beats furiously down upon the Americans in their intrenchments, drenching them with rain and benumbing them with cold. Still they hold their forts. At daybreak the stranded vessels are seen flying signals of distress. A heavy sea breaking on the shore forbids the idea of landing troops to-day; moreover, the American defences are now so strong that it would be madness to attempt to storm them.

The end is now felt to be near. A council of war decides upon the immediate evacuation of the town. The transfer of artillery, ammunition, and stores on board the shipping begins at once. The Tories, having first obtained leave to quit the town when the troops do, are packing up and wringing their hands. Very little of the accustomed hilarity is heard at the mess-tables. Household goods and merchandise of every sort are being hurried on board the transports. A general commotion and hubbub prevails, in the midst of which General Howe sends word to Washington that if allowed to embark his army unmolested he will leave the town uninjured.

Thus, in six days from the time the siege actually commenced, the possession of the New England capital is secured to our arms. It is true the Americans have been lying before it for eleven months, not as besiegers but as watch-dogs.

The remaining days of British occupation are to be signalized by disgraceful and wanton plundering by the British soldiery. By virtue of might the General takes possession of all the woollen and linen goods in the town. His soldiers break into and rob stores and dwellings at night, destroying what they cannot carry away. The streets are barricaded and scattered with crows-feet[1] to prevent a sudden rush of the rebels into town.

This state of things continues until the 17th, St. Patrick's day. And as this is the day dedicated to that saint who expelled all venomous creatures from Ireland, so shall it witness the expulsion of the army which for eleven months has devoured and laid our fair metropolis waste.

For after several futile attempts to get away, the Americans, determining to hasten their movements, have suddenly unmasked a battery on Nook's or Foster's Hill,[2] close to the water and holding entire command of Boston Neck and of the south part of the town. This notice to quit could no longer be neglected. This very step had been fear-

[1] An instrument with sharp iron prongs to hinder the movement of horsemen.
[2] Where the Lawrence Schoolhouse now is.

fully dreaded by the king's troops. Accordingly, by four in the morning, the army of subjugation began to embark; by ten it was all on board and under sail. The drums at Roxbury immediately beat to arms. At noon the selectmen came out of the deserted and plundered town to say that not a single redcoat remained in it. General Ward immediately mounted his horse and put himself at the head of Colonel Learned's battalion. General Putnam immediately embarked with a portion of his troops in the boats destined for the assault of the 5th.

The Continentals, with General Ward at their head, marched over the Neck to the British lines, that had so long hurled defiance, unbarred the gates, and picking their way through the *débris*, — dismounted cannon, broken tumbrils, camp-rubbish, and litter, — pursued their way quietly into the town.

The force under General Putnam landed at the foot of the Common. The two bodies together occupied all the important posts in the town, with Old Put as military commandant.

It is the peaceful Sabbath day on which these stirring scenes are taking place. Washington's order of the day is : —

"Parole St. Patrick, Countersign Boston."

Once more we stand in the deserted Province House. Nothing of the king except his arms over the door. Even the brazen Indian on the cupola, levelling his arrow, seems hastening the flight of the foe. Once more we enter the hallowed precincts of the Old South to find it — shame on them for the deed! — profaned by being turned into a riding-school for the British cavalry. Again, standing before the stately Town-House, memory recalls the splendid pageant of the imperial troops, flushed with pride, advancing to an easy conquest. Now that pride is in the dust. Pacing by the silent graveyard where Winthrop lies in his tomb, the phantom of the old governor seems announcing: —

"Behold my work! In the downfall of every tyranny, see the fruit of the tree which I planted so long ago! My struggle was for conscience, yours is for civil rights. Both have conquered. The Empire is dead. God save the Republic!"

INDEX.

Adams, Samuel, sketch of, 75-80.
Ancient and Honorable Artillery, 28, 124-126.
Andros, Sir Edmund, at Boston, 53; deposed, 59.

Blackstone, Rev. William, at Boston, 19, 20.
Boston, settled, 19-25; why so named, 22, 23; territorial divisions, 22; site of first church, 23; early houses, 25, 26; streets, 27: government, 27; customs of the people, 28-44; dress, 44, 45; money, 46; household furniture, etc., 47-50; revolution of 1689, 52; first Episcopal services, 55; tavern signs, 80-83; militia in 1775, 123, 124; bombarded, 247; recaptured. 262.
Boston Massacre, 94.
Boston Neck, described, 62-65; a battle-ground, 241-244.
Boston Port Bill, effect of, 95.
Boston Stone, 126, 127.
Bradstreet, Gov. Simon, reinstated in office, 58.
Brattle Street Church, parsonage, 92; location of church, 118.
Breed's Hill, fortified by mistake, 164; defences described, 170, 171.
Brown, Enoch, site of his house, 64.

Bunker Hill, *note*, 142; fortified, 162-168; battle described, 176-184.
Burgoyne, Gen. John, sets fire to Charlestown, 176.
Byles, Rev. Mather, anecdote of, 71, 72; his son, 142.

Cadets, 124.
Cambridge, camps and colleges, 192-202; Washington's headquarters, 209, 210; Old Watertown road, 221-222; Charles River bridge, 223; defences, 228.
Charlestown, settlement of, 19; its Indian and English names, 19; why abandoned, 20; Neck described, 164; heights fortified, 164-168.
Christ Church, a visit to, 139-142.
Church, Benjamin, arrested, 221.
Clinton, Gen. Sir Henry, at Bunker Hill, 181.
Common, the, in 1774, 101; British camp on, 101-108; burials on, 115; military execution, 115.
Copp's Hill, visited, 142-144; cannonade from, 176.

Dock Square in 1775, 118-120.
Dorchester, settled, 20; heights of, 161; fortified, 250-263.
Downer, Eliphalet's, duel, 226, 227.

INDEX.

Dudley, Gov. Thomas, 23; his house at Roxbury, 26, 240.

Everett, Gov. Edward, birthplace, *note*, 252.

Faneuil Hall, history of, 119-123.
Fort Hill, why so named, 24; assault and capture of the fort, 56-60.
Franklin, Benjamin, his birthplace, 81; residence, 127; at Cambridge, 217.
Frankland, Sir Charles, residence, 150.

Gage, Gen. Thomas, sketch of, 83-87.
Gates, Gen. Horatio, at Cambridge, 219.
Gardner, Col. Thomas, residence and death of, 229.
Granary Burying-Ground, 104.
Gruchy, Capt., his underground arch, 146, 147.
Gunpowder Plot, celebration of, in Boston, 131, 132.

Hancock, John, sketch of, 106, 107; mansion described, 108; commissions Gen. Washington, 203.
Harvard College, old halls, 196-202.
Hastings, Jonathan, 196.
Hollis Street Church, 71.
Howe, Gen. Sir William, succeeds Gage, 86; at Bunker Hill, 177, 180; evacuates Boston, 262.
Hull, John, 144.
Hutchinson, Ann, residence of, 88, 89.
Hutchinson, Gov. Thomas, 75; residence, 152, 153.

Indian names for Boston and contiguous places, 8.
Indians, inhabiting Boston Bay, 8; anecdotes illustrating their manners, 9-18.
Inman's House, 188.

Johnson, Isaac, at Boston, 21.

King's Chapel described, 89-91.
King's Chapel Burial-Ground, origin of, 21; noticed, 91, 92.
Knox, Gen. Henry, his bookstore, 94; brings the cannon, 216.
Knowlton, Col. Thomas, at Bunker Hill, 173.

Lee, Gen. Charles, described, 218.
Lexington, expedition to frustrated, 134-138, 139; incidents of, 223-227.
Liberty Tree, 66, 67.

Mather, Cotton, 143; *Increase*, 143; *Samuel*, 143. *See* 149, 150.
Maverick, Samuel, at East Boston, 19.

Nantasket, early settlement, *note*, 20.
Nelson, Capt. John, heads the revolution of 1689, 58, 59.
North Battery, the, location of, 148.
North Square, sketched, 149-155.

Old Court House, 92.
Old Prison, 92.
Old South, used for Episcopal worship, 55; Tea-Party meeting in, 72-75.
Oliver, Lieut.-Gov. Thomas, residence, 222.
Otis, James, 71.

Paddock's Mall, 104; his guns carried off, 112-114.
Parting Stone, The, 232.
Patterson's Post, 190.
Percy, Earl Hugh, headquarters, 105, 106.
Phips, Gov. Sir William, residence, 145, 146.
Pitcairn, Major John, *note*, 142, 154.
Pomeroy, Gen. Seth, at Bunker Hill, 174.
Prescott, Col. William, at Bunker Hill, 164, 182.
Prospect Hill, fortified, 187.

INDEX. 267

Province Charter, how obtained, 60 (read the chapter); 145.
Province House, description of, 82, 83.
Provincial Congress, described, 192.
Putnam, Gen. Israel, at Bunker Hill, 164, 171, 172, 173, 179, 183; fortifies Prospect Hill, 188, 189; commissioned, 204; selected to attack Boston, 247.
Putnam, Gen. Rufus, at Dorchester, 254.

Revere, Paul, *see* Green Dragon Tavern; residence, 153.
Roxbury, Meeting-House Hill, 232; camps and defences, 234-245.
Rumford, Count, 127.

Second Church, The, 149, 150.
Shirley, Gov. William, mansion-house, 251.
Stamp Act Riots, 67-70.
Stark, Gen. John, at Bunker Hill, 168, 172, 173; camp, 188.

Taverns, 63, 81-83; Green Dragon, 130-133; George Tavern burned, 244.

Tea-Party, account of, 73-76.
Thomas, Gen. John, quarters, 234, 235; leads the troops to Dorchester, 253.
Thompson, David, at Thompson's Island, 20.
Town-House (or Old State House), 93-96.
Trumbull, Col. John, at Cambridge, 216.

Walford, Thomas, at Charlestown, 19.
Ward, Gen. Artemas, headquarters, 194-196; commissioned, 204; at Roxbury, 230.
Warren, Gen. Joseph, at Bunker Hill, 174, 175; killed, 183; birthplace, 240.
Washington, Gen. George, takes command, 206; headquarters, 209; quells a mutiny, 214; his wife, 216; advances his lines, 245; at Dorchester Heights, 259; order of the day, 262.
Winter Hill, fortified, 188.
Winthrop, Gov. John, locates at Boston, 22; his house, 73.

www.ingramcontent.com/pod-product-compliance
Lightning Source LLC
Chambersburg PA
CBHW031955230426
43672CB00010B/2159